POETIC VOYAGES CORNWALL

Edited by Allison Dowse

First published in Great Britain in 2001 by
YOUNG WRITERS
Remus House,
Coltsfoot Drive,
Peterborough, PE2 9JX
Telephone (01733) 890066

HB ISBN 0 75433 294 2
SB ISBN 0 75433 295 0

FOREWORD

Young Writers was established in 1991 with the aim to promote creative writing in children, to make reading and writing poetry fun.

This year once again, proved to be a tremendous success with over 88,000 entries received nationwide.

The Poetic Voyages competition has shown us the high standard of work and effort that children are capable of today. It is a reflection of the teaching skills in schools, the enthusiasm and creativity they have injected into their pupils shines clearly within this anthology.

The task of selecting poems was therefore a difficult one but nevertheless, an enjoyable experience. We hope you are as pleased with the final selection in *Poetic Voyages Cornwall* as we are.

CONTENTS

Will Maxfield-Coote	20
Adam Earl	20
Imogen Rutherford	21
Stephanie Brown	22
Kelly Jewell	22
Amy Hutton	23
Rosie Bailey-Clark	23
Isabel Connell	24
Emma Clunie	24
Charlotte Tomlinson	25
Taylor Wearne	25
Lauren Carol Anne Kean	26
James Mark Sampson	26
Annest Swann	27
Amy O'Brien	27
Zanna Goldhawk	28
James Grant	28
Suzy Allen	29
Casey Wearne	29
Ben Cowburn	30
Felicity Chadwick	30
Jasmine McKay	31
Jordan Lewis Gambrill	31
Melicca Edwards	32
Rachel Ashurst	32
Ellen Freeman	33
Robert Hobin	33
Matthew Laity	34
Tom James	34

Barncoose CP School

Sara Jane Rose	35
Nicole Anne Avent	35
Christopher Lane	36
Adam Quintrell	36
Craig Bullen	36
Cheston Forster	37

Mount Charles School

Stefan Putt	70
Abby Newcombe & Hannah Matthews	70
Martine Tregunna & Sarah Matthews	71
Elisha Crowle	72
Elwyn Moreton	72
Esther Rich	73
Ciaran Ashton	73
Chloe Foster & Laura Green	74
Natalie Martin	74
Amy Hemingway & Rebekah Ansell	75

Mullion Primary School

Louise Matthews	76
Madeleine Claire Cuff	76
Guy Olliff	77
Anny Rice	78
Lewis Paul Gilbert	78
Holly Bennetts	79
Alan Luc Lieske	79
Sophie Enever	80
Tara Nuzum	80
Trystan Stock	81
Jethro Watson	81
Kimberley Smith	82
Rebecca Gilbert	82
Ben Thomas	83
Emily Furber	83
Lee James Marchant	84
William Sherlock	84

Mylor Bridge Primary School

Meriel Smith	85
Daniel Walls	85
Angus Saunders	86
Jonathan Epps	86
Poppy May Reid	87
James Brougham	87

Adam Tucker	87
Jamie Pikesley	88
Rebecca Vinnicombe	88
Samantha Sleeman	88
Barnaby Farnworth	89
Olivia French	89
Amelia Rigby-Jones	90
Jez Popperwell	90
Michael Farey	91
Emily Halvorsen	91
Hayley Timmins	92
Jordan Rose	92
Robert Bugden	92
Kathy Hammill	93
Neil Keeble	93
Misty Barratt	94
Kieran Czunys	94

Pendeen Primary School

Gareth Spencer	94
Sean Daws	95
Emma Selston	96
Kirsty Turney	97
Joshua Holmes	98
Rebecca Gummoe	99

Polruan CP School

Joshua Hadley	100
Jamie Bawden	100
Megan Castle	101
Charlene Lamy	101
Joseph Tomlin	102
Rhys Lamy	102
Jack Harris	103
Jasmine Libby	103
Mathew Beresford	104
Jessica May Palmer	104
Leigh Harris	105

The Poems

POOR VICTORIAN CHILD

I am tired and weak,
Walking up and down the street.
I am dying of thirst,
My heart is going to burst.
I haven't got any shoes or socks,
All I live in is a cardboard box.
I don't got to school,
My parents are poor,
So we go on the streets
Begging for more.
I'm cold and dirty,
So is my littler brother, Berty.
I walk the streets selling matches,
My feet are full of blisters and scratches.
I see some rich children playing with a toy,
I wish it was me
But I'm just a poor Victorian boy.

Jack Gilbert (10)
Alverton CP School

TOUCH

Touch! What can you feel?
The rough back of a bat in a tree.

Brown back of a huge horse.

Touch! What can you feel?
The smooth dolphin,
He's swimming in the sea.

The furry cat lying by the fire.

Jack Drew (8)
Alverton CP School

THE HAUNTED HOUSE

The haunted house was a shivering skeleton
Shivering, shivering, shivering through the night
Crumbling, crumbling, crash!

The phantoms in the hall
Were a herd of howling wolves
Howling through the night
Howling through the night
With the full moon
Shining, shining, shining.

The ghosts like a . . .
Flock of eagles swooping to and fro
Between the crumbling walls
Hooting, hooting, hooting.

Crumble, crumble, crash!

Laylah Cook (9)
Alverton CP School

THE HAUNTED SCHOOL

The teacher is a vampire,
Ghosts like mist in the air,
They live in the graves,
The grave is a creepy bed.
The teacher is a scary vampire,
With blood on his teeth.
The darkness is like a spook in the blanket.
The school is like an empty shell.
The children are scared of the teachers
Like mice scared of cats.

Jack Liddicoat (9)
Alverton CP School

MY DUMB CAT

I have a very dumb cat,
You may think I'm talking lies
But wait until you see him,
He brings in butterflies.
He brings in worms too
And from what I knew
He eats potato peelings.
I try not to hurt his feelings.

He fell into the fish tank
When the lid was closed.
He went all the way down
And sank like a bag of stones.
He was in the tumble dryer
And under the grill
And not very long ago
He fell off the window sill.

But still I love my cat to bits.

Rebecca Seymour (10)
Alverton CP School

TOUCH

Touch. What can you feel?
The slimy scales of a tremendous fish
Swimming in the sea.

Touch. What can you feel?
The spiny bark of a mighty oak tree,
The soft leaves brushing on me.

Eli-Joby Maeckelberghe-Jackson (8)
Alverton CP School

PINKEY

I love my little teddy,
She's the best teddy I know.
She's white and pink and pretty,
She'd come first in any show.

She has black and pink bright eyes,
With a really cute pink nose.
Her colours may be fading,
But she still has both her bows.

Her smile never disappears,
It will always be right there.
She's better than a rabbit,
Because she's a teddy bear.

She's small and cute and cuddly,
And so sweetly fluffy too.
On her feet it says, 'Love Me',
That's exactly what I do!

Jenna McCabe (10)
Alverton CP School

THE ANIMALS

Why do snow tigers live in the snow?
Why do rabbits dig holes?
How do giraffes have long necks?
Why do cheetahs run so fast?
How does the hyena get its name?
Why do elephants have trunks?
Why do koalas live in the trees?

Rachel Pratt (9)
Alverton CP School

BABY ANIMALS

Why do foals walk straight away?
Why do kittens purr and play?

Why do bunnies chew on grass and suckle from their mums?
Why do chicks peck at corn?

Why do piglets squeal and squeak?
Why do lambs jump and leap?

Why do joeys thump and punch?
Why do bear cubs steal fish from mum?

Why do puppies fetch a stick?
Why do kids butt and kick?

Rosie Kliskey (10)
Alverton CP School

THE ABANDONED SCHOOL

The silent bell rings!
Phantom children go to play!
Non-flesh caretakers float like a boat on water
Up and down the corridors.
Teachers in their classrooms
Like a ball bouncing backwards and forwards.
The bell rings again
The children come in through the walls
And not the doors
And they get taught by the teachers.
Everything's dead, even the spiders.
Dead!

Jophis Nutter (9)
Alverton CP School

DRIZZLE THE CAT

Her purr is a steam engine,
Speeding towards it destination.

Her mew is a baby,
Crying for her milk.

Her fur is a tiger's,
Camouflaged in the jungle.

Her eyes are fluorescent stars,
Sparkling in the dead of night.

Her paws are little white socks,
All fluffy and cosy.

Her tail is a snake,
Lashing out when in temper.

Kimberley McCreadie (11)
Alverton CP School

THE DOG

The dog is like a howling wolf
Calling for a friend.
The house was an empty shell
Standing still and alone.

The ghost is stomping around the house
Looking for its prey.
The house is like a creaking tree
Falling, falling, falling
Crash!

Harry Griffith (9)
Alverton CP School

THE WEATHER

Bang, crash, flashes of light
Through the bedroom window
I'm awake that's for certain
What an alarm clock,
Time to get up and get ready for school.
I draw back the curtain
And rain beats against the window
Like gravel beating against the window
The sky black, as night.
A big flash lights up my bedroom.
I jump into my bed and under the blankets
Frightened like a fox being chased down a hole by hounds.
I poke out my head from under my bed.
Bang, crash goes the thunder.
I'm staying in bed.

Ryan Holland (10)
Alverton CP School

THE HAUNTED CASTLE

The bed is like a dark, cold grave,
The crumbled walls are like a shipwreck under the sea.
The misty rooms are like a bomb shelter.
The whole castle is a massive quarry.
The front room is a tank of blood.
The door to the garden is locked forever.
The ruined pictures are on the floor, creeping behind you.
Swords flying through the air like a dragon's tail
Swishing round and round.

Scot Davies (9)
Alverton CP School

SKIING (INTRO)

Skiing is fun
It's also cool
When I was skiing
I wasn't at school.

The crispness of the morning snow,
Crunches under my feet wherever I go
And as the day turns into night,
The big full moon
Keeps the mountains bright.

Once safely tucked in my bed at night,
I ski over moguls as if in flight.
But now my skiing time must end
And I will keep in touch with my friends.
The mountain slopes give me no fear,
I shall be coming back next year.

Vashti Maeckelberghe-Jackson (10)
Alverton CP School

THE ANIMALS OF THE WORLD

How does the cheetah run so fast?
How did the hyena get its laugh?
Where did the lion get its paws?
Why does the bear have long claws?
Why does the elephant have such a long trunk?
What else has a smell like a skunk?
Why is a snake so fierce?
Why do we have deers
In this world?

Rebecca Goody (9)
Alverton CP School

THE THRILL OF THE FAIR

The lights that flash so high and bright,
And shine into the murky night.
The shouts and screams that fill the air,
From the thrill of being at the fair.
The rides go up, the rides go down,
They twist and turn round and round.
Hot dogs, burgers everywhere,
The smell of onions cooking there.
Candyfloss, toffee apples, sticky sweets,
Are all very nice to eat.
Goldfish and teddies galore,
All to win when you score four.
Then hush and quiet all around
As the fairground shuts its ground.

Kelsey McDonald (10)
Alverton CP School

THE HAUNTED SHIPWRECK

Beware, under the ocean there lays the haunted shipwreck.
It is dark and scary down there.
Do you dare?

The water was a smog of gas,
There are dead bodies and hidden treasure down there.
Do you dare?

But it is guarded by the haunted captain,
His beard is like a mouldy sponge.
Do you dare take the plunge?

Matthew Dennis (9)
Alverton CP School

THE FOOTBALL MATCH

The league game's drawing nearer
The fans are pouring in
The teams are getting ready
To beat their enemy
The manager's worst player
Sitting on the bench
He cost a tidy fee
To spearhead the attack
He's got to score today
To keep the team alive
Twelve games without a goal
His worst time in years
The team walks out onto the pitch
To see the awaiting crowd
The match kicks off
It's going well
The manager's worst player is coming up the pitch
And lines up his shot
It is hit or miss
He dodges a sliding tackle
And hits the ball with grace
It soars through the air
And hits the net with pace
The manager is delighted
Jumping up and down
His worst player has kept them in the league
He has scored at last
He has won the game.

Chris Roberts (10)
Alverton CP School

I AM EARTH AND YOU ARE SPACE

I am Earth and you are space,
Oh how I'd love to go there,
Such a wonderful place.

The stars are your eyes,
The universe is your face,
The planets going at blistering speed
While the Earth goes at a slow pace.

Your galaxies are beautiful
With many jet back holes,
Here people only value things
If it really glows.

Your comets are shining brightly,
They dash through the atmosphere.
We have lots of different weather,
Some that many fear.

I am Earth and you are space,
I have now finally been there,
An amazing galactic place.

Jocelyn Hutchison (10)
Alverton CP School

UNDER THE SEA

Under the sea the mermaids look up at you and me,
Under the sea fishes swirl around you and me.
Under the sea the sea urchins blow bubbles in and out
And hear us scream about and laugh and shout.
But when the day is over the sea has a party just like you and me.

Abigail Brown (10)
Alverton CP School

IF I WAS RICH

If I was rich
I would buy a car
and drive it far.

If I was rich
I would buy a bike
and go for a hike.

If I was rich
I would buy a surf board
and take it abroad.

If I was rich
I would buy a pool
and act very cool.

If I was rich
I would go on camp
and get very damp.

Ellis Hughes (10)
Alverton CP School

AT NIGHT

At night when the stars shine bright,
And the animals are sleeping,
I looked out of my window,
And saw two huge wings,
The trees swaying with the wind.
Then crash,
Trees falling, birds sing,
Shouting, screaming everywhere,
Shadows in every corner.

Ewan Witherow (10)
Alverton CP School

A LITTLE PONY

I know a little pony,
He lives just down the road.
His field always was my favourite place,
When I was little and unknown.

But when finally I grew up,
I forgot all about his field.
I went all the way into town,
To make myself pretty and unreal.

I walked back along his lane,
And happened to glance up.
I looked straight into that kind face of his,
And saw him staring back.

I love that little pony now,
He lives just down the road.
His field is my favourite place,
Now I'm big and well-known.

Katy Talbot (10)
Alverton CP School

THE WAVE

Rolling and growling like a tiger in the forest,
Fighting against the falling rocks,
No-one can fight with the deadly wave,
Fierce with blistering red eyes staring at you
Like the dragon of death.
People are screaming whenever they see the wave
Until suddenly it stops.
Everything stops forever.

Bianca Zambo (10)
Alverton CP School

THE TORNADO

The trees rustle,
the ground shakes.
A shiver runs
down your spine.

It pulls its way,
through the sky.
Creeping across
darkened land.

The air, a wind,
moonless night.
It rips
houses apart.

Leaves stop flying,
night, silent.
We're free and safe,
the beast has gone!

Charlotte Nicholls (11)
Alverton CP School

MUSIC

Music is a book,
Waiting to be read.
It tells a story,
Of magic and wonder.

Music is a spy,
Ready to unleash,
All its secrets,
And give you a picture.

Music makes you laugh,
Music makes you cry.
Sad, happy, strong or weak,
Music has a feeling.

Sinéad Connell (11)
Alverton CP School

BEEP!

Beep, that's all I hear
Beep, have no fear
Beep goes that car
Beep it went far
Beep, I am brown
Beep, I'm safe and sound
Beep, he said something bad
Beep, I feel very sad
Beep I have turned a bend
Beep, this is the end

Matthew Andrews (10)
Alverton CP School

FIREWORK NIGHT

The fire sparkling with flames,
Catherine wheels and rockets going off,
People eating hot dogs,
Colourful fireworks going *Bang! Crackle! Pop!*
Sparklers flashing about,
Stalls selling hot dogs and soup.

Jack E Rescorla (10)
Alverton CP School

DAD'S COOKING

Keep out of the kitchen - Dad's cooking!
Bet you can't guess what he does?
He burns sausages, lets the bacon go cold,
Drops egg shells on the floor,
Splatters brown sauce on the door.
The cooker buzzes, the microwave pings,
The smoke alarm bleeps.
Keep out of the kitchen - Dad's cooking!
But my dad cooks brilliant baked beans,
Makes perfect pepperoni pizza,
Fries fabulous fish cakes
While Mum burns the toast!

Benjamin Christopher Nowell (10)
Alverton CP School

SPITFIRE

Running along the runway like a bird,
Taking off, hovering,
A long, swooping dive-bomb!
Twirling!
Looking for prey.
At last he sees the enemy
And then comes in for the *attack!*

Like a charging missile!
He got him with one shot!
He turns for home
And disappears into the twilight!

Jacob Porter (10)
Alverton CP School

A WICKED DISGUISE

The referee is a lion
His beard is his mane
He stalks the pitch from side to side
In his 90 minutes of fame

He starts the match
With one loud blow
And ends it
With fans crying, 'No.'

To show the cards
He's not afraid
But in his job
He is well paid

He doesn't fear to argue
Or stop to change his mind
In fact he's rather vicious
Some say that he's unkind

They leave the pitch frustrated
All because of this one man
But a match without him
Would get quite out of hand

The players really hate him
They think he's really mad
But if they said this to his face
From football they'd be banned

Jessica Ross (11)
Alverton CP School

OUR TEACHER

Our Teacher is a monster
With six-inch fangs
A smile appears on his face
When the lunch bell bangs

He creeps up the hallway
And eyes up every child
Whatever meat, he does not mind
Tender, rare or mild

At lessons in the class
He hates children with a brain
He likes to find something hard
To cause them lots of pain

Near the end of the day
There's just me and my mate
He goes to the toilet
Just to find his fate

I'm now running home
To tell my mum and dad
About our monster teacher
Who's absolutely *mad!*

Richard Turner (10)
Alverton CP School

THE SEA

The sea's claw slams down on the shore
Scraping against each rock
Dragging back with it loose pebbles
It gives a huge and fierce roar

In its calmer moments the sea sways to the shore
Playing with the pebbles
It puts them in neat piles
And gives a soft and quiet murmur

Louise Hobin (11)
Alverton CP School

AZURE DREAMS

A mysterious past, origins unknown,
Rumours keep on growing and growing,
About the myth of that legendary dream,
Of course the dragon, Azure, dreams,
Since now and then people tried to unlock,
The ruined remains of the past time clock,
It seems no one knows if Azure did exist,
But still they tackle the time of mist.
Legend says Azure had stone crystal eyes,
Shining blue wings which he used to fly,
Did Azure's dreams sound like a fife?
Legend says so on its own life,
Was Azure slain by an unknown source?
Legend says not, he was an awesome force.
Just then those theories were fulfilled,
No, Azure's dreams could not be killed.
A fife-like sound pierced the air,
A body with eyes and a haunting glare.
The crystal eyes on the beautiful blue shape,
Everyone's mouths were widely agape.
That shape came to be our Azure dreams,
Once was that mystic legendary dream . . .

Poppy Stephenson (11)
Alverton CP School

THE GAME

The piercing whistle sounds
As the teams flood out

Boots smash in the puddingy mud
As players leap for the sailing ball

I catch the punching place kick
And run like the wind

'A noble try,' my team-mates shout
When I stand up past the touchline

More tries harvested
As the elephantine pack charges

A glaring error gives the ball on a plate
And our opponents score

A scalding look for the mistake
As the screaming ball converts the try

The sharp long peeps sound the end of play
It dawns on me that we've won.

Will Maxfield-Coote (11)
Alverton CP School

THE SEA

Sometimes when you're in your cabin it rocks us all to sleep.
Sometimes it grabs the fishing boats and grabs them down the deep.
The sea is like a roaring lion, it growls and bares its teeth,
The paw comes down and grabs the boat and pulls it underneath.
But the sea can be calm and bright and sparkling in the sun,
But when you're playing by the shore then it can be fun.

Adam Earl (10)
Alverton CP School

YELLOW DRAGON

Cheetah, cheetah running fast
Through the fields and through the grass
From the monster, an evil thing
When it's around the birds don't sing.
Its eyes that never blink
Tearing down trees before it does think.
The trees are falling, falling, falling.
What has happened to this world?

Rumble the sound is near
All the wildlife shake with fear
The yellow dragons are back again
They're only here to cause mayhem
Trembling, trembling at the sound
The forest lying on the ground
What has happened to the world?

Because of humans' selfish greed
They never think of what animals need
Houses, houses everywhere
The forest floors lying bare
Fumes and pollution
The sky will die
The black clouds begin to cry.

If nothing is done the Earth will be dead
So people try to use your head.
Help us, help us.
We're fading fast.

Fading, fading, fading fast.

Imogen Rutherford (10)
Alverton CP School

THE MAGICAL GALLOPING BLUE AND GREEN SEA

The sea is a lion, the waves are a herd of white horses,
Scar, the lion, roars down from the dark depths of the ocean,
White horses surf along the edge of the sea,
The lion finally gets tired and stretches his claws on steel hard rocks,
The big grisly bear covers the sky in total blackness,
The golden pony raises his head up to bright sunshine,
White horses once again gallop onto the beach,
Scar, the lion, grabs the white horses,
Slowly white horses dissolve into lovely shells,
The lion lets people on the beach,
Instead they swim in his precious sea,
But with horses' blinding whiteness he is distracted,
In time he goes out deeper to sea leaving people to enjoy the beach,
Beautiful white horses also go away,
Where to be found?
Instead Simba and brown horses take over the glorious kingdom,
'Come back,' say the people, 'come back.'

Stephanie Brown (11)
Alverton CP School

SEASONS

It's great all year with seasons going by,
With hot summer days that are always to be dry.
With snow in the winter
Where you can play and have fun,
And beautiful spring mornings
Where flowers blossom under the sun.
The autumn is chilly with trees that are bare,
And no more lying on the beach
- It isn't fair.

Kelly Jewell (10)
Alverton CP School

THE WORLD ALL AROUND ME

Listen
(What can you hear?)
The popping bubbles
In the bath.
Horses hooves
Clicking on the path.

Listen
(What can you hear?)
The hissing snake
In the deep dark sea.
The bright green pencil
Staring at me.

Amy Hutton (8)
Alverton CP School

WHAT ARE YOU LOOKING AT?

Look
What can you see?
A foggy faint shape of a faraway tree,
A tiny kitten sitting on my knee.

Look
What can you see?
A shabby dog tied to a lamp,
A crazy weirdo licking a stamp.

Rosie Bailey-Clark (8)
Alverton CP School

TOUCH

Touch
(What can you feel?)
The prickles of a hedgehog
Really hurting me.
The soft warm cat
Sitting on my knee.

Touch
(What can you feel?)
The slimy skin
Of a scaly fish.
The smooth bottom
Of a yellow dish.

Isabel Connell (8)
Alverton CP School

THE RAGE OF THE FOREST FIRE

It is a vicious red monster
Crackling and spitting
Eating everything in its path
Nothing left but dry bones moving slowly on
Never stopping as long as there is food
Never tired, doesn't need sleep
Air and wood as life
Water and stone as death
We all hear the scream
It's the end.

Emma Clunie (10)
Alverton CP School

WHAT A WORLD!

Touch
(What can you feel?)
A fluffy hamster
Scratching at me,
A creepy crawly crawling
Up to my knee.

Touch
(What can you feel?)
A rock hard house
In front of me,
I am going inside
To have my tea.

Charlotte Tomlinson (9)
Alverton CP School

LOOK

Look
(What can you see?)
The tiny brown tree trunk,
The little yellow seaside.

Look
(What can you see?)
The huge blue sea,
the small yellow bumblebee.

Taylor Wearne (8)
Alverton CP School

I LOVE SPRING

Look
What can you see?
A bright orange chick
Staring at me
And a black shiny crow
Sitting in an oak tree.

Look
What can you see?
A slippery dolphin
Splashing at me
And there at my front
A yellow bumblebee.

Look
What can you see?
Forget-me-nots and daisies
Standing in lines
Then I see a patch
Of brightly coloured vines.

Lauren Carol Anne Kean (8)
Alverton CP School

THE WEATHER

Sometimes the weather is bad,
Sometimes the weather is good,
But either way I'm happy.
When it's raining I go inside and watch the raindrops fall.
When it's sunny I buy an ice cream with my money.
And best of all when it's snowy
I build a snowman.

James Mark Sampson (10)
Alverton CP School

OUTSIDE

Look
(What can I see?)
A sparkling leaf
Floating from a tree,
A slimy old frog
Looking straight at me.

Look
(What can I see?)
A wrinkly teacher
Swimming in the sea,
The black and gold stripes
Of a bumblebee.

Annest Swann (8)
Alverton CP School

MY BED

Safe and cosy,
Warm and snug,
My bed feels like a little rug.
Sleeping soundly, curled up tight,
Nothing can get me in the night.
I sail away on my dream bed,
Across the oceans deep.
My pillow is a desert island,
Containing treasures sweet.
I rest my head upon its shores
As I splash my feet in deep, warm sleep . . . zzzzz . . .

Amy O'Brien (11)
Alverton CP School

WHAT CAN YOU THINK OF?

Think
What an idea!
A bright pink dog
Walking on the sea,
An exotic island
What a place to be.

Think
What an idea!
A deep blue skeleton
Driving a car,
A dark green moon
Next to a star.

Zanna Goldhawk (8)
Alverton CP School

WEATHER

The wind cries
The wind screams, it is a banshee
The wind howls as a hyena
The wind wails
The water laps the shore as a cat laps milk
The sea is roaring as a lion
The water rushes by
The trees arch their branches
The trees weep
And the clouds fly by like cotton wool

James Grant (11)
Alverton CP School

LOOK

Look
(What can you see?)
A dark green pencil
Staring at me,
A pretty bird
Sitting in a tree.

Look
(What can you see?)
Children playing
All around me,
People swimming
In the blue sea.

Suzy Allen (8)
Alverton CP School

SILENT

Listen
(What can you hear?)
The rattling leaves from a big oak tree,
The chatter, chatter, chatter, chatter
Of the singing birds,
The great fierce lion
Growling at me.

Listen
(What can you hear?)
The echoing mountains shouting at me,
The splashing of a river
Running at me.

Casey Wearne (8)
Alverton CP School

A NORMAL LIFE!

Look
(What can you see?)
A yellow chick
Blinking at me.
A scary lion
Roaring for its tea.

Look
(What can you see?)
Mum and dad
Drinking their tea.
A pitch-black cave
Full of bumblebees.

Ben Cowburn (8)
Alverton CP School

A SCARY NIGHT

Look!
(What can you see?)
A gloomy bat
Staring at us,
A hairy mouse
In an old haunted house.

Look!
(What can you see?)
A chocolate cake
Waiting for me,
Would you like
To come to tea?

Felicity Chadwick (8)
Alverton CP School

TOUCH

Touch
(What can you feel?)
The prickle of a hedgehog
Jumping on me.
The sharp, hot sting
Of a bumblebee.

Touch
(What can you feel?)
The slimy skin
Of a scaly slug.
The smooth, soft feel
Of a rabbit's nose.

Jasmine McKay (8)
Alverton CP School

LOOK

Look
(What can you see?)
A strict teacher staring at me.
A feathery bird
In a sycamore tree.

Look
(What can you see?)
My best friend
Walking up to me.
A scaly fish
Swimming in the sea.

Jordan Lewis Gambrill (8)
Alverton CP School

LOOK

Look
(What can you see?)
A lady in a house
Having some tea.
A dog on a beach
Swimming in the sea.

Look
(What can you see?)
A white and black dog
Climbing up a tree.
My mum and dad
Swimming in the sea.

Melicca Edwards (8)
Alverton CP School

LOOK!

Look
(What can you see?)
Beautiful red roses
Sitting in the ground.
Lots of tiny posies
Spread out around.

Look
(What can you see?)
A sparkling star
In the black night sky.
A colourful butterfly
Fluttering by.

Rachel Ashurst (8)
Alverton CP School

LISTEN, WHAT CAN YOU HEAR?

Listen
(What can you hear?)
A buzz, buzz, buzzing
Of a bumblebee
The chatter, chatter, chatter
Of a chimpanzee.

Listen
(What can you hear?)
A fierce lion
Roaring at me
A tweeting bird
In a faraway tree.

Ellen Freeman (8)
Alverton CP School

LOOK AND LISTEN

Look
(What can you see?)
A brown baboon
Sitting in a tree.
A blazing sun
Smiling at me.

Listen
(What can you hear?)
An ancient man
Calling to me.
A whistling creature
From the sea.

Robert Hobin (8)
Alverton CP School

MY DREAM

Look
(What can you see?)
A huge fearsome lion
Roaring at me
A big furry cat
Up a sycamore tree

Look
(What can you see?)
The big blue sea
Playing with me
The big yellow sun
Smiling at me.

Matthew Laity (8)
Alverton CP School

LOOK

Look
(What can you see?)
The colour of an apple
Gleaming at me
A hooting owl
Sitting in a tree

Look
(What can you see?)
A dark black slug
Staring at me
The bright green grass
Swaying in the wind.

Tom James (8)
Alverton CP School

THE BLACK CAT

There once was a cat,
Very black cat,
He was big, fat and fluffy,
He had big, green, shiny eyes
That shone like diamonds in the sky,
And his tail was long and curly,
He used to curl up in his basket,
In front of a big log fire,
And oh his big soft ears used to perk,
As he was always very alert,
And he was certainly very nosy,
But he loved his home,
Even when he was there all alone,
He thought it was very warm and cosy.

Sara Jane Rose (9)
Barncoose CP School

THE HORSE

Trotting fast down the lane,
Turning each and every corner.
Galloping up and down the steep hill,
Rocks scattered everywhere.
The noise of rivers running past you,
Birds tweeting from high up in the branches.
Rabbits running across the road like cheetahs,
Stomp, stomp over the molehills,
Yum, yum, some juicy grass.

Nicole Anne Avent (9)
Barncoose CP School

MY DOG JED

Dogs are good, sometimes they're bad,
Our dog Jed is completely mad.
When he's told to sit he stands up tall.
When he's told to lay he runs for his ball.
When he's out in the field he loves to run
And chases his tail in the morning sun.
When we get home, it's time for tea,
A bone for Jed and some chips for me.

Christopher Lane (9)
Barncoose CP School

THROUGH THE TUBES

Out the house,
Into the tubes.
He goes red,
He goes blue.
He goes yellow,
He's out of his tubes,
And into his house.

Adam Quintrell (9)
Barncoose CP School

MY PUPPY

My puppy called Muffy,
Went for a walk in the park,
He fell in a puddle and got scruffy,
Then ran all the way home in the dark.

Craig Bullen (9)
Barncoose CP School

THE PLUG HOLE

Here I am, sitting in the bath minding my own business
When suddenly, I started shrinking.
It was like I was floating in the sea.
I was being sucked to the end of the bath.
I felt like I was sliding down the water pipe.
I was.
Down, down, down I went until I reached the sewers.
It was dark, damp and smelly.
There was all sorts of rubbish down there.
There was crisp packets, cola cans, plastic bags.
I was washed through the sewers and out into the sea.
There I sat, floating on a wooden board
Hoping someone would save me and take me home.
That's another poetic voyage.

Cheston Forster (9)
Barncoose CP School

RIVER VOYAGE

Down I trickle with the mountain stream,
Meandering like a slippery, slimy snake,
Covering the ground like a little girl's ribbon,
Starting to gather in pace.
Down I flow, tunnelling under a bridge
Like a mole underground.
I start to grow bigger and burst my banks.
I have little streams joining me and flowing by my side.
Suddenly down I fall like raindrops falling from the sky.
The waterfall pushes me out into the estuary,
Out into the salty sea.

Alice Fruer-Denham (10)
Calstock Primary School

RIVER VOYAGE

River flowing down and down
Making just a whooshing sound
As it passes the slithery meanders
Up above people play rounders.
Tributaries are like youngsters
Leading down to one big river.
In the summer there are boat races
Going over Plymouth and places.
The source is at Woolly Moors
Where it hardly ever pours!
It's a lovely colour of muddy brown
Horrible colour it sounds.
My journey ends at Plymouth Sound.

Joseph Drabble (10)
Calstock Primary School

THE RIVER TAMAR

I am a river,
I start in the Barrows,
Then I go flowing down to the sea,
I see many things on my way,
Bridges, boats and quays,
As I flow I meander,
Into the Plymouth Sound estuary,
Reaching my mum,
The sea.

Sam Pascoe (10)
Calstock Primary School

RIVER VOYAGE

Slimy, slithery, squelchy,
But still as beautiful as a bluebell wood,
Gliding down from the source,
Meeting tributaries like the forks of a tree,
Rippling, rolling round and round,
A tiger running and roaring,
Meandering around houses and trees,
Starting to flow and ebb and get a tide,
Coming out at the river's mouth -
The mouth of freedom,
The mouth of sound,
The mouth filled with salt and seagulls,
Freedom - the sea!

Jos Kirkman (11)
Calstock Primary School

RIVER VOYAGE

My source is at Woolley Moore
Meandering around rocks and towns,
Catching my mother's raindrops.
A tributary meets me halfway through my journey.
Ships going up and down,
Taking goods throughout the county,
Bridges going across me,
Tunnels built beneath me.
Sometimes I flood all along the river.
My mother is at Plymouth,
Finally I meet her
And my journey starts all over again.

Alex Glover (10)
Calstock Primary School

RIVER VOYAGE

I circulate on the River Tamar from the source.
I say to myself I've got a course to tackle.
I trickle down from Woolley Barrows.
I glide down past Vinworthy.
Rushing up and down meanders.
Ripples tickling my tummy and drifting,
Tributaries leading me astray.
I whirl and swirl for forty-seven miles from my source to mouth.
My icy cold, murky brown water flows down hills and valleys.
My tide pushes me more and more.
I drift down towards the salty sea,
Where my voyage ends.
My fortune is beyond the horizon.

Freddy Luesby (11)
Calstock Primary School

RIVER VOYAGE

Rivers on their voyage to the sea.
They run down from their source.
They run fast; they run slow.
They grow from small to big.
They meander round sharp bends
They twist; they turn.
Finally out of the mouth into the sea.
We're *'free'*.

Taro Tollitt (9)
Calstock Primary School

RIVER VOYAGE

The river crashes against the boat
The wind howls against my coat
The sails are flapping
The roof is tapping
The sea is mad
The wind is bad
Then it stops
The river's silent
Everywhere is quiet
The sun came out
The birds tweet
There was no wind beneath my feet.

Celia Ivey (10)
Calstock Primary School

SOMEWHERE IN OUR WORLD TODAY . . .

Somewhere in our world today
a joyful game of hockey was suddenly being ended by the lazy referee.
Somewhere in our world today
a little girl nonchalantly woke an adult.
Somewhere in our world today
dying people starve loudly.
Somewhere in our world today
dopey William was daydreaming very quietly
while the *evil* teacher spoke loudly.
Somewhere in our world today
tired Adam fell asleep extremely quickly.

Adam Hendra (10)
Crowan Junior & Infants School

THE COW

A smooth jumper
A bad listener
A wild eater
A swift runner
A head rubber
A smelly animal
A skidder
A non-flyer

Gavin Tregenza (9)
Crowan Junior & Infants School

A TANKA

I'm disappointed
You were doing so well on
Your surfing but you
Ruined it by giving up
And you were one of the best

Luke Clancey (10)
Crowan Junior & Infants School

A CHICKEN

A laying machine
A pecking beast
A food Hoover
A quick mover
A feathered wing
A clucking hen

Joe Pawluk (9)
Crowan Junior & Infants School

THE LION

A magnificent predator
A silent stalker
A majestic runner
A swift leaper
A lazy sleeper
A deafening roarer
A territorial attacker
A proud beast

Josh Bates (10)
Crowan Junior & Infants School

A TANKA

Exasperated!
I watch as they torture her.
It makes me so sick.
So I shout for a teacher.
They are scared like their victims.

Josie Hall (11)
Crowan Junior & Infants School

A TANKA

I feel so lonesome
I hate loneliness, don't you?
Ever been alone?
I hate it, it's like being
Locked away . . . and being left.

Hannah Butcher (10)
Crowan Junior & Infants School

SOMEWHERE IN OUR WORLD TODAY

Somewhere in our world today
sleeping poor people are painfully dying of thirst.

Somewhere in our world today
three people are greedily eating in the lunch break.

Somewhere in our world today
twenty-nine people in a class are quietly working.

Somewhere in our world today
we are dreaming about disgusting monsters.

Somewhere in our world today
a lonely person is sadly working.

Tom Spires (10)
Crowan Junior & Infants School

SOMEWHERE IN OUR SCHOOL TODAY . . .

A bunch of rosy children are absorbed in another world
with Roald Dahl in the library.
Some five-year-olds are happily munching away
in our hall down the long, windy corridor.
Twenty-six jolly pupils are in a marathon down to the classroom doors
except for one miserable little girl named Jennifer Cotten
who walks pigeon-toed, one foot in front of the other.
As she plods along you can often hear her soggy boots squelching
as she slowly walks up to the teacher's classroom
where everyone will be waiting patiently for her.

Nina Philp (11)
Crowan Junior & Infants School

SOMEWHERE IN OUR SCHOOL TODAY

Somewhere in our school today
cool kids have a lot of fun

Somewhere in our school today
a silly boy is daydreaming very slowly

Somewhere in our school today
happy girls madly play netball
while two small boys have a large fallout

Somewhere in our school today
sleepy teachers have a long break
at the end of the day

Jonathan Barclay (10)
Crowan Junior & Infants School

SOMEWHERE IN OUR WORLD TODAY

Somewhere in our world today
A rapidly flowing river burst its waterlogged banks causing total havoc.

Somewhere in our world today
Two young men viciously assaulted an elderly woman.

Somewhere in our world today
A group of ten-year-old children
Are happily practising for their Christmas concert

Somewhere in our world today
A boy called Simon wrote this.

Simon Vincent (11)
Crowan Junior & Infants School

THE BUDGIE

A tiny thing
A fluffy chap
A yellow beak
A feathery back
A pretty face
A blue boy
A small tail
A little squeak

Jessica Green (10)
Crowan Junior & Infants School

LION

A furry giant
A quick killer
A swift mover
A high jumper
A meat eater
A silent creeper
A non-flyer
A great roar

William Masterton (10)
Crowan Junior & Infants School

SOMEWHERE IN OUR WORLD TODAY!

A class of cheerful children
were laughing very loud.

Twenty-four naughty infants
were shouting at the teacher.

Six angry teachers
are quickly getting mad.

Two frightening dinner ladies
are wildly flinging plates at each other.

Alexander Hickey (9)
Crowan Junior & Infants School

MY RABBIT

A small ball
A high jumper
A silent mover
A cute pet
A carrot chewer
A little devil
A thick coat
A furry tail

Aaron Kemp (11)
Crowan Junior & Infants School

MY MONKEY

A naughty fellow
A cheeky swinger
A tree jumper
A banana muncher
A hairy coat
An arm floater
A tail hooker
A forest hunter

Louis Goss (10)
Crowan Junior & Infants School

THE DOLPHIN

A smooth skin
A swift glider
A high jumper
A strong swimmer
A graceful twister
A beautiful chatter
A sailor's friend
A smiling eye

Emma Goodship (10)
Crowan Junior & Infants School

DOLPHIN

A fast swimmer
An underwater human
A fish chomper
A non-speaker
A big stomach
A fin slasher
A brilliant colour
A loving animal

Savannah Goss (9)
Crowan Junior & Infants School

SOMEWHERE IN OUR SCHOOL TODAY

Somewhere in our school today
A class of groovy, crazy children were coolly writing.

Somewhere in our school today
Twenty-four nasty infants
Were rudely being really horrible to the teacher.

Somewhere in our school today
Seven angry, grumpy children were improving their maths.

Somewhere in our school today
Crazy Mrs Carpenter was sneakily watching television.

Sharnelle Wyatt
Crowan Junior & Infants School

MY PUPPY

A fur lump
A devil eater
A bone chomper
A cat killer
A big nuzzler
A fond swimmer
A beach lover
A fast runner

Frances Anguish (9)
Crowan Junior & Infants School

MY DOG

A skinny stick
A fast mover
A sturdy thing
A hazel smell
A harsh bark
A sausage layer
A scared baby
A big dreamer
A great lover

Samantha Tonkin (11)
Crowan Junior & Infants School

VIEW OF A WHALE

A soft colour
A silky cloak
A small hole
A big splash
A deep sea
A fat creature
A big eater
A sometimes killer

Chloe Woolley (10)
Crowan Junior & Infants School

I LICKED A LOLLY WHEN I SAW POLLY

I licked a lolly,
when I saw Polly.

I did a big jump,
when my dad had a bike pump.

I went to a town and saw a load of eyes,
I ran back home and baked a lot of pies.

I ate all the pies up,
when people where having sup.

Then It was bed time,
but everybody was at a pantomime.

I saw a little girl,
with a big curl.

Rhiannon Paul (7)
Gwinear Primary School

IF YOU WANT TO SEE A TIGER

If you want to see a tiger
You must go down to the spooky, dark, cold jungle
You must go down there, you must.

I know a tiger who's living down there
He's a-huge, he's a-snappy, he's a-runner
He's a-cool tiger, yes he is.

Yes, if you really want to see a tiger
You must go down to the spooky, dark, cold jungle
You must go down there, you must.

Go down smoothly to the jungle and say,
'Tiger, dada, tiger dada, tiger dadaaaa,'
And out he'll jump
But don't stick around, jump in a tree.

Zac Jones (8)
Gwinear Primary School

IF YOU WANT TO SEE A TIGER

If you want to see a tiger
you must go down to the lost creepy jungle.
I know a tiger who's living down there.
He's a big, he's a mean, he's a fierce, he's a green.
Yes, if you really want to see a tiger
you must go down to the lost creepy jungle.
Go down gently to that jungle and say,
'Tiger mama, tiger mama, tiger mamaaaa,'
and out he will pop!
But don't stay, *run!*

Oliver Spence (7)
Gwinear Primary School

WINTER'S HERE

Winter's here
The skies are filled with ice
The hedges filled with frost
Sun sparkling like glass
The grass gleaming
When will spring be here again?

Ben Curnow (10)
Gwinear Primary School

VALENTINE'S DAY

Look at
The love around
Caring for the others
Presents and chocolate for your love
Today

Zac Smart (10)
Gwinear Primary School

MY BIRTHDAY

Hooray my birthday,
All the presents just for me
Wrapped in all colours,
Teddy bears with hearts on them,
What presents will I have next?

Sarah Norman (10)
Gwinear Primary School

CATS

Cats are small
Cats are big
Cats are thin
Cats are fat

What size are cats?

Cats are black
Cats are white
Cats are tabby
Cats are tabby and white

How many colours do cats have?

Cats live outside
Cats live inside
Cats live in and out
Cats live everywhere

Where do cats live?

C-C-C-C
Cats

Rowan Louise Todd (7)
Gwinear Primary School

SUMMER

Glance up.
Up at the sun,
Summer upon the beach,
See the children in the water
Playing!

Emily Phillis (11)
Gwinear Primary School

A PANTOUM

Tall and towering it used to be,
In the air a musty smell,
Crumbling down through all the years,
Mud surrounds it like a moat.

In the air a musty smell,
Sky seeping in through the stones,
Crumbling down through all the years,
Moss-covered like the hills.

Sky seeping in through all the years,
Nearby stands a chimney,
Moss-covered like the hills,
Big boulders piled high.

Stephanie Tregenza (10)
Gwinear Primary School

PIRATE CAPTAIN MASH

'Jump overboard,' says Pirate Mash.
'But, Captain Mash, I'll get a rash.'
'Then you must be the lookout.'
'But, Captain Mash, I cannot shout.'
'Then you must scrub the deck.'
'But, Captain Mash, I'll hurt my neck.'
'Then a pirate captain you must be.'
'Thank you, Mash,' says Captain me.

Cameron Neil Irish (8)
Gwinear Primary School

IF YOU WANT TO SEE A TIGER

If you want to see a tiger
You must go to the driest end of the Indian jungle

I know a tiger who is living down there
He is tiny, he is sharp-eyed
He is fast, he is terrifying

Yes, if you really want to see a tiger
You must go to the driest end of the Indian jungle
And say, 'Come out, come out, wherever you are,'
And up he will come
But don't stay, run away!

Sam Phillis (7)
Gwinear Primary School

NIGHT AND DAY

In the moonlight
Shining bright
The trees dance in the wind

The stars look down
On the town
The children are asleep

When tomorrow comes
Up jump the mums
And the silence drifts away.

Kate Hopkins (9)
Gwinear Primary School

ALL THE ANIMALS

One oyster oohing
Two tortoises trotting
Three thrushes thinking
Four foxes fighting
Five fishes flipping
Six snakes slipping
Seven snipes snipping
Eight eagles eating
Nine naughty newts nibbling noodles
Ten tigers tiptoeing
Eleven evil elephants eating
Twelve T-Rex's tapping their toes.

Rebecca Jill Pollock (8)
Gwinear Primary School

ONE OSTRICH ACTING ODD

One ostrich acting odd
Two travellers talking together
Three twerps threatening toddlers
Four fatsoes farting frantically
Five Frankensteins feeling funny
Six squirming silly snakes
Seven squirting Spanish spacemen
Eight elephants eating eggs
Nine naughty netasiss eating noodles
Ten teddies tickling Tom

Nathan Mark Bawden (9)
Gwinear Primary School

PETER LANYON'S COASTAL JOURNEY

A fish's home,
A bubbly bath!

A patchwork quilt,
A desolate farm!

A grassy tepee,
A home giver!

A rocky tower,
An ancient monument!

Rachel Trewartha (10)
Gwinear Primary School

THE WINDOW

The same window,
That same window,
I look right out,
Over the balcony,
I see the garden,
Weed-covered,
Only one plant surviving,
Being surrounded by a scruffy hedge,
Overlooked by a harbour wall,
The sea crashing against the wall,
People getting wet,
Hearing the stones crashing together,
All the boats bobbing up and down,
The boats clashing together,
Seagulls landing on the boats.

Gary Hill (11)
Landewednack Primary School

THE WINDOW

The same window,
That same window again,
I lean right out,

The scent of the jasmine hits me,
The hens and the chicks are out for a walk,
The pigs are eating quickly and the tabby cat is sleeping,

The tall oak tree stands deserted,
The bushes glisten in the morning dew,
The sharp grass blows in the breeze,

The sky is clear and the sun is blazing hot,
The church is ringing its bells,
The graveyard stays still as a doornail.

Amy Pitman (10)
Landewednack Primary School

THE WONDERS OF LIFE IN A WINDOW

The same window
That same window
A spirit of a fisherman looks out of a window.
From his cabin window he sees -
The sparkling water then the fierce waves crashing against the rocks.
He sees fish darting hither and thither like flashing thunderbolts.
He sees a fisherman fishing contentedly.
He hears a sea shanty chanting in his head.
He hears the whistling cry of the sea.
He hears the wind whistling through his grave.
He smells the fresh English air.
He smells the smell of fish hanging in the cabin.
He smells the wonders of life.

Paul Burgess (10)
Landewednack Primary School

THE VOYAGE OF LIFE

You walk the walk of life
The voyage of life,
Until you take the path
To Heaven.

Life is a gift you have only once
So enjoy it, it's a long journey
That lasts many years,
From young to old.

It has many happy times
And as many bad times,
It's not perfect
But it's yours.

Gail Kessell (11)
Landewednack Primary School

THE RIDE OF DEATH

Quick, run for your seat,
Hold on tight,
The ride is about to start,
Now close your eyes,
We're going up,
Up to the sky,
Round the corner,
Now we can fly,
Why did I get on his ride?
It is not what I thought,
Not one bit,
Stop it at once!

Rebecca Goodway (11)
Landewednack Primary School

I LOOKED OUT

The same window,
That same window again,
I lean right out . . .

I see a village,
So far out there,
With windmills tall,
They whip the air.

I look out,
And up above,
I see blue and white,
A heavenly sight.

Close to me,
I see the sea,
The dolphins leaping,
Wave to me.

I look again,
I see the boast,
They bob around,
And each one floats.

A cliff I see,
With gorse and tree,
Where seagulls sit,
And stare at me.

Even closer,
I see a glow,
The light it shines,
Around us so.

If you look closely,
You will see,
Some of these things,
Just like me.

Camilla Hawkings (10)
Landewednack Primary School

A WINDOW

I look out the window
The same window again
I see cars driving past
In a hurry to get places,
I hear children laughing
In the park,
I smell the smoke
From the nearby factory.

I see skyscrapers,
As tall as can be,
I hear the wind
Whistling in my ears,
I smell the cakes
From the bakery next door.
I see the Millennium Eye
Going round and round,
I hear birds crying
In the distance,
I smell the gas fumes from afar.

Catherine Allinson (10)
Landewednack Primary School

A WINDOW

I close my eyes . . .
It's that same window again,
And as I gaze out I see things
That I hadn't noticed before,
I see the palm trees waving in the breeze.
I see the cool welcoming turquoise sea
As the sun highlights it with liquid gold
And I can smell the scent of a tempting barbecue.
As I lean right out I hear the cry of excited children
Brought to me by the wind
And finally I see a small fishing boat sailing in the sunset . . .
Then I open my eyes,
I fight hard to hold on to my dream
But it's already gone.
No more can I smell a barbecue but now the scent of petrol,
My fishing boat has gone,
So has my golden sunset.
As I lean out of my clear-glazed mahogany window
My gaze falls on the busy town of London
And I remember how welcoming the sand had been.
I sigh, it's a shame dreams don't last.

Victoria E A Trott (11)
Landewednack Primary School

THE WINDOW

The same window
That same window again
I lean right out

To see my cat walking across the garden
The leaves falling off the trees
And to hear the bushes rustling in the wind

To see the seagulls flying across the cliffs
The fish swimming in the sea
The lighthouse flashing its light for miles

To see the boats picking up their nets
The buoys bobbing up and down
The dolphins moving in and out.

Robert Johns (11)
Landewednack Primary School

BUBBLES

I am a bubble.
People are looking at me outside in the street
As I float in the air in the sky.
I hover like a cloud.
I am a clever bubble.
I move in the air.
I can draw shapes in the sky.
I am floating.
I am small and big.
I am a smiling bubble.
Some bubbles bump into me.
I can draw heart shapes.
It is windy and cold.
I wish I was in the warm place.
I see a rainbow.
It is a coloured rainbow.
I am happy today.
Pop! Bang! Pop! Bang!

Chloë Habgood (7)
Launceston CP School

BUBBLES

I'm blown out.
My friends drift off and . . .
I'm alone on my own.
People try popping me
But I float away.
People look in me and my friend.
They see their reflection.
The cold is like snow.
I blow around.
The trees are blowing leaves nearly hitting me
And I nearly pop.
Dogs try catching me.
My friends and I are very colourful and bright.
That's why we're good fun.
I'm green, blue and purple.
Pink is the favourite.
Now I am leaving my friends.
Now I go
Bang!

Melanie Hatch (7)
Launceston CP School

BUBBLES

Bubbles, bubbles, you pleasant bubbles
With your beautiful colours.
When you dance about you reflect like a shiny car.
You glide like a bird.
People try to catch you but they never do so.
You travel overseas without knowing you are scared of a bird.
When you glide like a bird you look like a jet chopper flying over trees.
You reflect like a shiny dew.

Johnny Conway (8)
Launceston CP School

BUBBLES

'Yippee,' I said when I came out of the pot of bubbles.
How nice it is to be with other bubbles.
Big ones, small ones, like different planets.
As if I was a bouncy balloon in the high bright sky.
Wow! Look at the other colourful bubbles up in the sky.
As my journey begins I start to learn what is going to happen to me.
Ooohhh! Someone has popped another bubble, how scary!
Soon I shake and start to greet my partner that vibrates.
Now I have no fear to go near a child or two.
I have a mate to keep me warm inside from dusk to dawn.
I start to wrinkle like an old man.
I start to jingle like bells.
I start to quiver like an iceberg.
Suddenly! Pop!
Like raindrops. It's the end of my life.

Charlotte Clogg (8)
Launceston CP School

BUBBLES

Bubbles are different colours like a rainbow.
Bubbles pop and bang like a storm with lightning.
Bubbles can be different sizes, little and big and round.
Bubbles look like fairies glittering in the air.
Bubbles can float in the sky.
You can float like bubbles.
Bubbles are cool.
Bubbles bounce and bounce and bounce like a ball.
The bubbles disappear into the air.

Rhys Stevenson (7)
Launceston CP School

BUBBLES

I came through a stick.
I am very delicate with a mirror on my chest.
I flew to my friends.
How pretty you are.
My friends are really kind to me.
Me and my friends play hide and seek.
I hide behind a tree, the wind blew me away.
I shouted, 'Help!'
My friends tried to save me.
They blew away but all I heard was Help! Help! Help!
Pop! went one. *Pop!* went one. *Pop! w*ent another.
I shook and wriggled a little.
My colours grew mouldy,
All purple and goldy.
I hovered into a great, great field.
I went down and down.
I hit some spiky wire.
Ouch!
Water splashes out like a water volcano.
I am no longer a colourful bubble.

Stephen James Downing (8)
Launceston CP School

BUBBLES

Bubbles being popped and caught by a strange thing.
Bubbles that look like Minnie Mouse.
Bubbles yellow, pink, purple and gold like the sun.
Bubbles like igloos.
Bubbles walking in the air.
Bubbles dancing with lovely clothes on.
Bubbles big, bubbles small, bubbles all sizes.
Bubbles writing names in the sky.
Bubbles kissing.
Bubbles like stars floating in the air.
Bubbles pop like fireworks with a loud *bang!*
Bubbles don't want to go away.
Pop!

Sinetta Bond-Webber (7)
Launceston CP School

BUBBLES

I'm a bubble and I'm gliding over people's heads.
I'm floating towards a school.
In the school I saw my reflection in the window.
I saw other bubbles making words and names,
So I flew to them.
A bubble kisses me,
I bounce off it.
I'm floating back home now.
Pop!
I cry and die to go to Bubble Heaven.

Elliot Reece Jane (7)
Launceston CP School

BUBBLES

I float along by every roof and wall.
I fly as my friends pop one by one.
I am like a crystal.
My colours of orange, pink, yellow and blue flash brightly.
I glide like a bird, but children try to catch me.
I am too fast and high for them.
I move on.
I start to float down to the ground,
And touch the flowers that I had found.
I prance and dance along.
I'm going to die.
Ow, ow, goodbye, goodbye.
But I must have a short life you know.

Amy Lauren Trevethan (8)
Launceston CP School

BUBBLE

I am a bubble.
I float over the bushes and trees.
I can see people watching me.
Bang!
I shine like a lollipop.
Other bubbles swirl around me.
Some bubbles bounce on the floor.
I can float in the air.
I look like a ball.
I am going to hit the ground.
It's the end of me.

Catherine Diebner (7)
Launceston CP School

BUBBLES

I am floating high up in the sky.
I am going to die soon.
My friends are all around me.
They come where I go and my friends pop!
I pop where I touch.
I leave a wet patch all around.
I dance all day and silently float in the air.
I have colours inside me.
I like air.
I like floating.
People like watching me.
People blow me.
People like me.
There are lots of bubbles in the breeze.
I touch the wall.
Pop! Pop!

Natasha Smith (7)
Launceston CP School

BUBBLES

It floats into its adventure.
It starts strong and becomes weaker and weaker.
Big, small, all different sizes.
It hovered into a big kiss
That lasted for ages and ages.
People try popping it with their shining nails.
It's fading, faster and faster.
It's like an explosion.
Bang!
It's dead on a branch.

Eliot Astles (7)
Launceston CP School

JOURNEY TO THE GARDEN

Beds, wardrobes, chests of drawers,
Lazy Dad is sleeping,
Bedtime for my sister,
Down the stairs I am creeping,

Through the towering sofas,
Tables, chairs and lamps,
All obstacles in the way,
Even my old gramps!

Kitchen tables, knives and spoons,
My mum's cooking a cake,
Washing machines, tumble dryers,
What else is Mum going to make,

At last I am in the garden,
Time to find my prey,
Better be really quick
Or else I'll have to pay!

Stefan Putt (10)
Mount Charles School

JOURNEY TO OUTER SPACE

We're trying to find a spaceship,
For going to outer space,
We can't find hardly anything,
Only bits of lace.

At last we made a spaceship,
We had a bit of help from dad,
It shot up to the sky,
Our engine was quite bad.

There weren't many aliens,
On the planet Mars,
It was very weird,
And they didn't drive cars.

We're nearly at the end of the journey,
It wasn't very good,
Now it's midnight,
So don't wake the neighbourhood.

Abby Newcombe & Hannah Matthews (10)
Mount Charles School

JOURNEY TO THE SEA
(The Water Cycle)

We evaporated from the sea, we went up in little droplets,
We formed into a big cloud, when we got really big it started to rain,
We landed on a leaf, when it got full we started to drip,
We rolled down into a river, we got stuck in a reservoir,
Someone turned the tap on, and we came rolling through,
After they used us we went down the plug,
Deep into the sewers,
We swished through a machine to get sparkly clean,
   Now we start
      again!

Martine Tregunna & Sarah Matthews (9)
Mount Charles School

WHISKY AND THE STORM

Whisky the whale was swept out in the sea,
His mother cried, 'Oh where can he be?'
Whisky was drowning because of the storm,
He was near New Zealand by the time it was dawn.
In the Indian Ocean he still carried on,
He looked for his mother but he knew she was gone.
He swam on past Brazil and saw hunters that kill,
He swam to South Africa and then Madagascar.
He found his way home and his sisters and brothers,
But he never did find his beautiful mother.

Some fishermen say
That they heard one day,
Whisky's mother calling,
They followed her cry,
But they never did find
Whisky's beautiful mother!

Elisha Crowle (10)
Mount Charles School

THE FLY

Zoom, zoom, zoom,
Flying round the room
Smell of sugar, *yum!*
Nice sticky buns
Whoosh, of wind rushing past
Hand comes down, *crash!*
Shoo, shoo, fly away
Out, out, up and away
I live to see another day.

Elwyn Moreton (8)
Mount Charles School

JOURNEY TO GRANDMA'S!

Grandma and her house are pretty much the same,
They're both old and dirty! Definitely not tame.
So one day mum says,
'Oh yes, yes I know what to do,
We'll go and visit grandma.'
'Thanks, Mum, I *really* love you!'
Some have pretty grandmas, some are even *rich!*
Mine is old and haggard and reminds me of a witch.
'Oh no!' cried mum, 'I've lost the map.'
Then I had an idea.
'I know the way, I'll tell you.'
(Yes I will tell her, in a year.)
'Are you sure?'
'I'm sure, I'm sure, Mum!'
'Left, right, forward, *turn!*' I wasn't dumb,
I wouldn't just let her drag me away to grandma's,
So I'd help her to get lost hoping we'd turn up at grandpa's.

Esther Rich (10)
Mount Charles School

THE SALMON

The journey of the salmon begins in the cold, deep ocean.
Past an enormous monster with eight legs, swims the salmon.
Nets, flesh-eating fish and man-made machines avoided by the salmon.
The change from salt water to fresh water,
From surf to flowing stream is sensed by the salmon.
Against narrowing riverbanks and rising currents, fights the salmon.
Over raging white water and plummeting falls, leaps the salmon.
And finally, in the stillness of the spawning ground,
Rests in peace, the salmon.

Ciaran Ashton (10)
Mount Charles School

JOURNEY AROUND THE FACE

Deep beneath the blood and cells,
Lives a brain all lumpy and bumpy.
Next come the eyes,
The nice blue eyes,
Blinking and winking,
That's what they do.
Here we have the pointy, long, sniffing nose,
Now comes the munching, crunching teeth,
Next come the chatting lips.
Oh no! We're going into the mouth,
To the wiggly tongue.
Ahh! Help!

Chloe Foster & Laura Green (10)
Mount Charles School

AEROPLANE

All you can hear is a loud roaring noise,
From the engine spluttering loud,
A wonderful plane is soaring,
And flying into a cloud!
I look outside the window,
What a wonderful view!
For fields stretching endlessly,
And the seas are glistening blue,
I turn my head from the window,
For the engine is starting to slow.
I know I'll remember this journey,
I hope there's more to go!

Natalie Martin (10)
Mount Charles School

OUR JOURNEY TO EARTH

We're coming in our spaceship,
It's a bumpy ride.
My alien friend does not like it,
Because it smells inside.

We're going to take over,
The planet will be ours.
We've been travelling for hours,
From the planet Mars.

We've landed on a supermarket,
Grannies are rushing by.
They look so very queer,
Now we've got to fly.

Oh no, we're lost,
The engine has gone wrong.
Bang! Bang! Crash! Crash!
Our boot had a bomb.

We saw the president,
We blew him up, he twirled.
We had our weapons ready,
So we took over the world.

Amy Hemingway & Rebekah Ansell (10)
Mount Charles School

MOVING ON

My childhood life left behind,
With all the years and tears of joy and sadness.
My friends and foes sad to say goodbye to a friend after times of fun.
All the things I leave behind, to come and find sea, sand and sun.
Such fun I had,
But now I'm sad to say farewell to my home.

A fresh start, a new place, new people and friends to meet.
Just thoughts to have and thoughts to think;
Yet the memories still remain,
Finding toys and games I used to play brings tears to my eyes.
Words of hope and joy help me along,
But regret for what I left remains in my heart.

New things and sights, people to meet and talk to,
New things to do and hope for.
If I keep a brave face, smile and laugh,
Hope to please and not feel too sad.
I hope to return when I'm older, to see my friends,
To see how much they have changed.
Life will have changed by then and me with it,
Who knows what the future will be like?

Louise Matthews (11)
Mullion Primary School

STAR GALAXY

Steal the mist from a crystal ball,
Then mix it with a moonbeam lotion.
Take a pinch of a redbrick wall
And add it to the potion.

Now you're really on your way,
But there's a few more things
You can't delay!

Hook a star from above
Then reel it in with care
Make sure it's one you really love
And that your choice is fair.

Make a knot of the blackest night
Then slip it in a jar
Now mix these things with all your might
And throw it really far.

Madeleine Claire Cuff (11)
Mullion Primary School

IN A CAT-LIKE STORM

In a slashing cat of a storm
There is but just one life-form
Sailing along in his boat

'Go back to shore,' cried the stormy brew
''Tis night, I only have a few
O' fish to feed my wife and me, not you.'

''Tis I will give you fish
But ye have to give me a wish.
The thing I need's a tommy
To suit not you but me.'

'Here is your tommy.'
'Thank ye, thank ye.'
'Oh person thank ye
By putting ye on the rock.'

'Help me! Help me!'
'Ah but you gave me the key
To use you as bait.'

Guy Olliff (10)
Mullion Primary School

I HAD A LITTLE SMILE

I had a little smile
And I kept it in a tub
I got it out every day
It enjoyed a tummy rub
Then one day I realised
I could use my little smile
So I slapped it on my face
And it lasted for a long, long while
I went outside
And chucked my tub into a bin
Then I saw someone in the street
And gave him a little grin
He then started smiling
As he carried on down the road
He gave the smile to someone else
Is this the start of a special code?
So if you have a smile
Don't keep it locked away
If you give the smile to someone else
The whole world might smile some day

Anny Rice (10)
Mullion Primary School

WHITE HORSES

White horses gallop fast,
Look at that one going past,
Tore a hole in our boat,
But we're still afloat.

Huge wave hit again,
'Help, help,' we said to a plane,
Tore another in our boat,
But we're still afloat.

Big horse out in front,
Smashed through with a thump,
It's torn another in our boat,
But now we cannot stay afloat.

Lewis Paul Gilbert (11)
Mullion Primary School

A RECIPE FOR A RAINBOW

To make a rainbow first you need,
a round yellow pumpkin seed.
Then add one litre of juiced blueberries,
next a handful of round red cherries.
Spoon in five winter-size drops of rain,
whilst blending in a handful of orange grain.
Now your mixture is nearly done,
but don't forget a blaze of sun.
Next you will see light shining through,
and that's your rainbow created for you.

Holly Bennetts (11)
Mullion Primary School

A DREAM

Stir in a thought
And roll it out taut
Drop in a child
In a warm cosy bed
Pour in a colour, maybe some red
Then mix for a while and leave to set
And once you've done
Have a little fun.

Alan Luc Lieske (10)
Mullion Primary School

ME ... AND THE SEA

      The sun,
    the sea,
the sand,

I now,
    put out,
        my hand,

        to catch,
    the waves,
of the sea,

to be,
    no one,
        except me.

Sophie Enever (10)
Mullion Primary School

A WISH

All you need is one black night
a shiny star
and the brightest light
then take a rose petal
and leave it to settle.

Find a bumblebee's wing
maybe a cloud
and a strong wasp's sting
mix it together
then stick in a feather.

Bake until ripe
then it should be ready
within the smoke of a pipe.
I hope it's been fun
because now it is done.

Tara Nuzum (11)
Mullion Primary School

A DRAGON

Take a cup of gold and silver,
Stir around for a minute or two,
Then that's the skin,
Take two misty wonder balls,
Now your mixture's almost done,
But don't forget a fine flame,
Now my friend, our potion's done!
Just leave to stand in the midday sun.

Trystan Stock (10)
Mullion Primary School

RECIPE FOR A STAR

Take a shimmer from the moon
Add a flower blooming in June
Whip in some dark milky mist
From here we'll continue the list
Throw in some black from the dark of the night
And sprinkle in a touch of light
And now our star will glow with might
I hope you've made this star with delight

Jethro Watson (10)
Mullion Primary School

HOW TO MAKE A RAINBOW

A pinch of bright lights
A sprinkling of sparkling colours
Flowing into the dark nights.
Grab the moon all big and round
Just one fluffy big white cloud
Steal a blend of sun and rain
And a handful of grain
Whisk until shining
There's a whining *bang!*
You're left with a rainbow.

Kimberley Smith (10)
Mullion Primary School

TO MAKE A RAINBOW

Steal the redness of a fire,
the peeling from an orange,
heat from sun
Yet you've only just begun.
The blush of a cheek,
blue off a beak
green from the grass,
and the violet from the past.
Now you are left with a rainbow.

Rebecca Gilbert (10)
Mullion Primary School

A RECIPE FOR A LAUGH

Take a tub of a dolphin's squeak
Add in a pinch of a bird's beak
Sprinkle a bit of glittering sun
Slice in half a creamy ice bun
Pour in a scaly fish's dive
Take a dash from a honey-coloured beehive
Steal a barrel of rum
Then fold in a baboon's pink bum
Now we have finished our recipe for a laugh
So now you can take a relaxing bath.

Ben Thomas (10)
Mullion Primary School

MY SPIRIT

My spirit is alive and happy,
but lies in those memories,
in those ashes of joy, happiness, dying and death.
My eyes will not open tomorrow,
nor the next day,
never again,
I am dead,
but my spirit is alive,
alive and happy,
and will live on.

Emily Furber (11)
Mullion Primary School

TO MAKE A COMET

Start with some fire,
To build the heat up higher,
Throw in some iron,
As strong as a lion,
Add the breath of a dragon,
And the wheel of a wagon,
Chuck in some sandpaper to make it all rough,
Then toss in some steel to make it tough,
Crush up a boulder,
Then leave it to smoulder,
Now throw it up,
Into the sky.

Lee James Marchant (9)
Mullion Primary School

LIFE AND DEATH

The fierce ferocious hurricane
Was throwing the houses around like playthings,
And the world was spinning, spinning, spinning
Like it was never going to end.

The spilling hurricane was eating cars,
And ripping trees from their roots,
And they were flung for millions of miles.

William Sherlock (10)
Mullion Primary School

THE SEA

The sea is a tabby cat,
Rolling and tumbling, stalking its prey,
So huge and wonderfully stripy,
Rushing to the shore,
As if it's chasing a mouse,
Lapping at the shore,
As if it's drinking milk.

Hiding behind monstrous cliffs,
Little cowardly waves wait,
But when there's a boat out at sea,
The sea's a tiger, a lion, a leopard,
Battling with its prey.

He cracks rocks to pieces,
Or sleeps gently on the shore,
Always unpredictable,
Always changing,
Either a restless panther,
Or a tiny kitten.

Meriel Smith (9)
Mylor Bridge Primary School

AUTUMN TREES

Green brown leaves rustle,
Swirling in the air like birds,
Crunchy, dry, they die

Daniel Walls (8)
Mylor Bridge Primary School

LIGHTNING

The lightning is like an eagle
Looking for its prey
He swoops down quickly
And rips it to pieces
Carrying it far away

In the night
It scrapes its claws on the windows
And tries to get in
Making a din!

The next day it has gone
It doesn't leave a trace
It has left us
Will it ever return
And come back to this place?

Angus Saunders (8)
Mylor Bridge Primary School

THE CREEK

1 boy writing a poem
2 oyster shells covered in seaweed
3 boats waiting on the shore
4 ducks paddling by
5 trees blowing in the wind
6 lumpy pieces of slippery seaweed
7 seagulls arching in the sky
8 coloured buoys bobbing in the water
What a busy place!

Jonathan Epps (8)
Mylor Bridge Primary School

THE SUN

The sun is like a lion
Pouncing after you
Burning leaves and plants
Making everything go crisp, crunchy and brown

Roaring like thunder in the heat
And killing everything in its path
Clouds cover the sun
The flowers are closing
Ready for winter to come
And the lion goes to sleep.

Poppy May Reid (8)
Mylor Bridge Primary School

THE SEA IN THE CREEK

Browny, green ripples
Rushing quickly into shore
Bringing in the tide

James Brougham (8)
Mylor Bridge Primary School

THE SCHOOL POND

Dark pond full of frogs
Water skaters zooming by
What a place to live

Adam Tucker (8)
Mylor Bridge Primary School

THE MINOTAUR STORM

The storm is like a monstrous Minotaur
Searching for his meal
He swiftly glides down
Brushing everything out of the way
It bashes at the trees and bushes
Then it rushes furiously away
To return another day

Jamie Pikesley (9)
Mylor Bridge Primary School

THE SNOW

The snow comes down floating doves.
Covering the Earth with white feathers.
It floats gently down.
Making no sound.
It settles with no noise.
Bringing fun for girls and boys.

Rebecca Vinnicombe (8)
Mylor Bridge Primary School

A CLOUD

A cloud is made of cotton wool,
When snow comes the fluff falls
When rain is falling
Little pieces of fluff fall down
And turn into water on the ground.

Samantha Sleeman (8)
Mylor Bridge Primary School

THE LIGHTNING

The lightning strikes the Earth
Like a demented jaguar
His forked tongue
Like a cobra snatching its prey
Killing everything in its way
Murdering trees
With every strike
Finding people and stabbing them
With all its might
So
Be careful
He's after you

Barnaby Farnworth (8)
Mylor Bridge Primary School

THE WIND

The wind is a dog
Rushing down the road
Never still as a log
But howling as it goes

And at night when all is quiet
The sky is dark and tired
He comes out to run round riot
Covering everything with a breeze

But later the next morning
All is still
The wind is barely yawning
Over the hill

Olivia French (9)
Mylor Bridge Primary School

THE WARLOCK

The brother I have is small but weird,
A few days ago he really disappeared.
Not in the night no! Nothing *like* that,
He disappeared right in front of me, and my cat!
He said, 'Dilly dallyu and dang woof doo,'
And he disappeared like a supersonic Winnie the Pooh!
Before that he was just an ordinary boy,
With pointed ears, and the greenest eye.
Well, once before, I swear I say him *fly!*
He jumped off the stairway and boy, did he whiz,
Then he stopped flapping arms and wings he grew,
Well, I started to think that is very new!
Then he clapped his hands and flew back down,
Even though he landed in the middle of town!
Oh dear, I was worried, what to do!
Wait, listen, what is the flapping at the window?
Why, it's my little warlock brother Ben,
And he has come home again!

Amelia Rigby-Jones (8)
Mylor Bridge Primary School

BURNING RED SUN

A tiger burning in the sky
Hot as ever be
Angry red roaring eyes
On the burning angry tiger.

Racing round the bend
Silently sniffing on a slippery stream
Sending down its burning beams.

Jez Popperwell (8)
Mylor Bridge Primary School

THE AVALANCHE

The snow speeds like a cheetah
Racing to kill the leaping mountain goats
The cheetah crawls, then races and zooms
To defeat its prey.

The snow floats and lands like an albatross
Gigantic wings cover the mountains
With soft white feathers.

The sun kills the snow
Like a deadly scorpion
With his dangerous sting
Winning the battle of the seasons.

Michael Farey (9)
Mylor Bridge Primary School

SNOWDOG

There was a snowdog
In the middle of the snow
He made our fingers glow

The next day
He came back looking nice
And covering everything with ice

Then came the rainy man
The frosty snowdog he found
Turning him to slush on the ground

Emily Halvorsen (9)
Mylor Bridge Primary School

THE SUN

The sun comes out and brightens up the sky,
It looks more like a light princess
With a bright yellow dress
And wearing a golden crown,
When the day is nearly over
The princess goes away
But she will come to play another day

Hayley Timmins (8)
Mylor Bridge Primary School

THE SEA AT NIGHT

Is a crushing lion
Bashing and swirling rocks
Wrecking a ship in a bite
Lashing against caves
Knocking down cliffs
Searching for its prey
That may come its way.

Jordan Rose (8)
Mylor Bridge Primary School

LIGHTNING STORM

Lightning is a shocker
It has over 10,000 volts
Go quickly or it'll be a locker
It might even shock all the bolts.

Lightning is like a python
Suddenly it snatches its prey
It jolts out of the sky
Before it flashes a sigh.

Robert Bugden (9)
Mylor Bridge Primary School

THE HAIL

The hail comes down
Like big huge boulders
Crashing cars and bashing roofs
Hitting people on the head
Disturbing others who are in bed
It looks like white ping pong balls
Crushing towns and villages as they fall.

Kathy Hammill (9)
Mylor Bridge Primary School

SNOW

Snow comes down
Like frosty white leaves
It comes like a frosty boat
Making frosty streams
And frozen pipes
Car wheels get stuck in the snow
No water, just ice
That's snowy weather.

Neil Keeble (10)
Mylor Bridge Primary School

RAIN RAT

The rain is like a rain rat
Grey and wet
Splashing down from the sky
Rattling on the windows
Making a flood
Lashing down the road
Rolling and growling
Creeping up to the house
With its sharp claws

Misty Barratt (9)
Mylor Bridge Primary School

EARLY EVENING SKY

I see the light moon
The clouds are moving slowly
Brightly shines the sun

Kieran Czunys (9)
Mylor Bridge Primary School

SUPERMARKET TALE

And they're off
To a spine-chilling start
Now the contestants
Are Mr Moo and Mrs Bright
Oh look Mr Moo is off to an uddering start!
But Mrs Bright is running faster than light.

A tin of meat
Is toppling to his feet
Shoving in tins of this and tins of that
Almost running over a cat

Speeding round the first corner
Waving to a school friend, Lorna
Bending, turning, zigging, zagging
Speeding through the finishing flagging.

Gareth Spencer (10)
Pendeen Primary School

GOING SOUTH

Gliding through the air
Feathers everywhere
Hovering above France
People look like ants
Flapping wings, left and right
Day has gone, in comes night
Landing on a big oak tree
Little birds staring at me
Cold weather still ahead
Little children wrapped up in bed
Birds are going south for winter
Fences icy about to splinter
Slipping through the sky
As slick as a zooming fly.

Sean Daws (11)
Pendeen Primary School

THE ORPHAN'S VOYAGE

Orphan on a filthy train
Cloudy sky, drizzling rain
Where is she going to go?
Being passed to and fro
People talking to each other
Orphan wished she had a mother.

Under a tunnel and over a hill
Orphan shivers, she's got a chill
The rain stops, the sun comes out
But all she can hear
Is the ticket man's shout

Time to get off and onto the ferry
She is sad but everyone's merry
Pouring with soaking rain
Onto the ferry and off the train

The ferry leaves at 8 o'clock
Sailing away from the dock
The orphan cries and walks away
And the sun sets for the break of day

The orphan decides to go to sleep
She throws herself in a careless heap
Sleeping in a squeaky bed
And a duck-feathered pillow for her head

Waking up really early
It wasn't time to got up surely?
Getting dressed, freezing cold
The sun shining bright and bold
Off the old and onto the new
Sailing upon the ocean blue.

Emma Selston (10)
Pendeen Primary School

SUPERMARKET SWEEP

And she's off
Rushing to get the soaking wet trolley
She's in the supermarket
Throwing the potatoes into the bag
But, oh dear
A potato has fallen onto the floor!
But she doesn't care
She's rushing to the tomatoes
She's putting them in a bag
Now she's off to the milk
Putting one in with care
1.6 seconds
She's the fastest one we've had
Up to now
She's off to the cold butter
And grabbing the ham as well
She's in the next aisle
Throwing in the cheese
She's rushing to the onions
She's rushing three aisles ahead
Picking up four tins
Of garden peas and baked beans
Throwing in the crisps and cola
Looking at the wine
Picking up the red and white wine
Through the checkout
2.10 seconds
She's the fastest one we've had.

Kirsty Turney (10)
Pendeen Primary School

A ROAM THROUGH THE FOREST

I turned my jog into a pace
As a cold wind spread along my face
I walked past the leafless trees
Rusty hinges in my knees

I walked further into the forest
Ahead of me stood a door
I stretched my hand for the handle
A dim light shone from a candle

A rotten hand had reached out
It was over I had to shout
I screamed it out
The weird creature stumbled back

Where he landed I do not know
The creature had gone in a cloud of smoke
The trees of black stumble back
I listened hard for a noise

An ear-splitting crack
A shiver down my skinny back
The ground absorbed my shaking feet
I had slipped into the final sleep . . .

Joshua Holmes (10)
Pendeen Primary School

THE PARK

In the middle of a city
There stood an enormous park
We sometimes go there
Even in the dark.

We sometimes take a picnic
And we sit on a giant stone
My mum is always with me
So I am never on my own.

I like to jump in the water
We walk along the very long path
We throw stones into the pond
And we like to take a nice hot bath.

We go on the big stepping stones
And I have a lot of fun
I swing on a huge tree branch
And sometimes we have a cream bun.

While my mum picks lovely flowers
I go on the swinging bar
Sometimes my hand slips
I see a blue toy car.

Nearly every time we go to the park
We always meet someone we know
Sometimes we talked to each other
My friend wears a pretty pink bow.

Rebecca Gummoe (11)
Pendeen Primary School

OWL

His wings as silver
He spreads with pride
His tummy rough and grey
For all his prey.

For the day is long when he sleeps
But in the evening
The owl's mystical powers
Are set free
In the street and in the forest.
His eyes are midnight blue
His wings are as soft as snow
But all the time you're thinking
'He's catching something to eat.'

In the night he uses his magnifying sight to soar
And with his piercing talons
He takes his victim to eat.

For the night is long as well:
That is what I call the owl's time:
The great bird that is beautiful and mysterious.

Joshua Hadley (10)
Polruan CP School

OWL POEM

Eyes big, searching for prey mice and rats.
Claws for catching, sharp, to grip prey.
Wings for soaring.
Beak for killing and eating.
He returns to the free dawn to sleep.
The next night he hunts again.

Jamie Bawden (10)
Polruan CP School

TAWNY OWL

I have fluffy, flapping wings,
Which stretch out so far,
I glide across the sky.

With big, beady brown eyes,
I can see the distant fields.

With my talons I catch my prey,
Small mice scuttling,
So when I catch them I can tear them up.

I have an orange beak,
So I can eat my prey.

Guessed what I am?
That's right
I am a *tawny owl!*

Megan Castle (10)
Polruan CP School

MY BARN OWL POEM

I am a large brown owl,
Soaring through the starlit sky.
I have large beady eyes to help me search for prey.

I have soft, fluffy wings to help me stay up high,
And fly across the countryside.

I have sharp, grippy claws
To help me pick up the animals I eat.

I have a sharp, pointing beak
Piercing the prey.

Charlene Lamy (11)
Polruan CP School

OWL

Big, beady eyes for searching,
Searching for food to eat.

Big feathery wings to fly,
Flying to catch his food for tea.

Claws, sharp claws to catch his prey,
Catching prey to survive.

Owls fly at night,
Being nocturnal allows them to catch mice,
Mice come out at night
Not forgetting voles.

Joseph Tomlin (8)
Polruan CP School

OWL POEM

An owl with big eyes,
In the dark,
Sleeping and creeping,
Watching the park,
Out comes the rat,
Owl pounces and eats it,
His wings carry him,
Soaring round the park,
He returns to his tree.

Rhys Lamy (10)
Polruan CP School

THE OWL

His fragile wings
Are sleek and soft
With a ruffled look
He spreads his wings with pride

His staring eyes
Are large and wide
That shift nervously -
They search with pride

His powerful talons
Are sharp and shiny
That grip tightly -
They catch with pride

This nocturnal bird
Is graceful and gentle
And proud

Jack Harris (11)
Polruan CP School

OWL

Big eyes shine in the dark
Watching out for mice and shrew.
When he sees mice or shrew
He'll flap his big wings,
Get his prey and fly away.
When the owl returns to his nest,
He'll eat his prey
Holding it down with his razor-sharp claws.

Jasmine Libby (9)
Polruan CP School

THE OWL

Big, round immense eyes
Searching for prey such as mice and voles.

Fluffy sleek feathers help him fly
Help him fly through the night sky
Slowly drifting, not making a sound.

Vile claws pierce the victim
Slashing away with his beak.

The victim falls into the deep dark stomach of the owl.

Mathew Beresford (9)
Polruan CP School

OWL

Big, brown, winking eyes looking for my food.
When I see something that I like I do not take my eyes off it.

I love my big brown wings
They're really helpful when catching my prey
And they are essential to keep my babies warm.

I have long curly claws
And they grasp the mouse as I pounce.
I grip the branches.

Jessica May Palmer (10)
Polruan CP School

MY BARN OWL

The claws are sharp to grab prey
When the prey tries to escape it can't.

The owl flies back to the nest
He gives the prey to the babies.

The wings are big and brown
When he flaps it gives a gust of wind.

The beak is sharp
It grips its prey and swallows it whole.

Big, beady eyes to watch its prey
He does not let it out of his sight.

Leigh Harris (9)
Polruan CP School

OWL

Big, brown winking eyes
Watching out for prey.
I see something good to eat
I don't let it out of my sight.
I flap my smooth wings
Gliding through the air.
With all the stars and a big bright moon
I fly away to my nest
And hope to come back soon.

Sara Parfitt (10)
Polruan CP School

OWL

His belly is big,
From eating and eating.
He eats small creatures,
So that's why he's big,
But he carries on eating.

His eyes are shut at day but not night,
When he catches his prey using his sight.

His talons are sharp,
To pierce his prey,
He may also use them in a fray.

His wings are strong, they beat with great power,
He flies through the sky,
And catches his prey,
And then uses his wings to return home again.

His beak is as sharp as the head of an arrow,
He uses it to swallow and rip up his prey,
Sharp but gently he feeds his demanding young,
Regurgitating pellets are evidence the meal is over.

Laurie Russell (10)
Polruan CP School

LIMERICK

There was a young girl called Nicky,
She had a lolly that was very sticky,
It fell on the ground,
With mud all around,
She picked it up and gave it to Vicky.

Danielle James (9)
St Columb Major Primary School, St Columb

CLOUDS

Fluffy white shapes
Up there in the sky,
A pillow for me
It will be mine.

Sticky candyfloss
Dropped in a puddle,
Lost there forever
Longing for a cuddle.

The thick black duvet
Has pulled over the clouds,
They've gone to sleep
Like I have now.

Sophie Perry (10)
St Columb Major Primary School, St Columb

MY CAT TOBY

Compared to all other cats,
My cat is the best.
Toby is black and white,
Like a zebra crossing,
His golden collar shines like the sun.
In the summer
Toby chases flies and butterflies.
Jumping in the air,
Paws clawing,
He looks so silly.
He scratches me a lot,
Probably because I tease him!

Martin Pearce (10)
St Columb Major Primary School, St Columb

BONFIRE NIGHT

Bonfire night can be a fright.
The *whizz* and *fizz* gets people in a tizz.
Rockets *zoom* and *boom*
Loud enough to shake the room.
Bonfires *hissing,*
Fireworks *sizzling,*
Catherine wheels spinning,
Starts all the children grinning.
Fireworks shoot up high
Bang!
Silver and gold pennies all over the sky.
It's the end of the show,
And it's time to go.
Some children are very happy,
But some are tired and *snappy.*
Our cheeks glow red,
It's time for home and bed.

Jamie Varcoe (11)
St Columb Major Primary School, St Columb

MY BLACK CAT

I have a cat named Spice,
She is so very nice,
Her eyes are green,
Her smile is slightly mean,
Her claws are sharp like blades
And her fur is black as a witch's cat.
You won't see her on a broomstick,
But inside as snug as a bug on the rug by the fire!

Jessica Bonney (9)
St Columb Major Primary School, St Columb

RUBY

Ruby is cute,
She is a springer spaniel.
Ruby is white with brown blotches.
She is 18 months old.
Ruby is energetic and lots of fun,
She plays games with all her toys.
Ruby never seems to get tired.
She is my dog and I love her.

Ruby is cute,
She chases her tail.
Ruby likes to go for walks,
She likes to run in fields.
Ruby eats up all her food,
She likes bones the best.
Ruby is my best friend,
She is my dog and I love her.

Joanna Powell (9)
St Columb Major Primary School, St Columb

MY BEST FRIEND

My best friend is called Joanna.
She has blonde hair and blue eyes.
She is quite small.
She is nearly always happy but sometimes gets angry.
Her favourite food is mashed potato.
She likes most games.
She is like a cuddly teddy.
She is my best friend.

Gemma Wall (9)
St Columb Major Primary School, St Columb

TIC AND TAC

Tic is nine,
Tac is ten,
They are mine,
They live in my den.

They swim around,
As fast as can be,
They are like hounds,
I hope you see.

They are orange and white,
With lots of spots,
They like the light,
They live by the clock.

They are always there
To comfort me,
I always treat them with care,
I love them and they love me!

Jenna Rundle (10)
St Columb Major Primary School, St Columb

STARS

Stars are bright,
They twinkle through the night,
Some are shiny,
Some are tiny,
I wish I could touch a star,
But up there is too far!

Hayley Davies (9)
St Columb Major Primary School, St Columb

MY OLD HOUSE

My old house was *haunted!*
Every time I crept up the hall
A chill travelled down my spine.
My mum became scared too.
She slept downstairs!
My sister didn't care,
She was only young.
I didn't like it one little bit.
I could hear strange noises.
Like boos! And crashes! And slams!
And one night I heard a very sharp
Ear-piercing scream!
That was two houses ago,
We moved from that place
But the chilly thoughts
Still bring goose pimples to my skin.

Vicky Sztajnert (10)
St Columb Major Primary School, St Columb

THE GHOST

A gust of nothingness,
Floating by,
Giving you an eerie feeling in your bones.
A sheet of dampness,
The moon making it shine.
A translucent mist rising up slowly,
From the waterfall of death.
A mad cloud of evilness,
Searching for a new body.
Bored with tedious death.

Lauren Watson (11)
St Columb Major Primary School, St Columb

MY BED

Every night,
I snuggle into my bed,
With my TV on,
Holding onto my ted.

My mum comes up,
And says, 'Goodnight,'
Goes out of the room,
And switches off the light.

As soon as the bulb goes out,
I listen to the wind,
I hide under my soft covers,
And have a little cringe.

I suddenly fall asleep,
With my cat on my bed,
Then wake up in the morning,
Looking at the sun gleaming red.

Jody Barnes (11)
St Columb Major Primary School, St Columb

MY TEACHER

Do this, do that
He seems to like picking on me,
His laugh makes me so irritated.
He has some good points
Like the games he plays,
And the easy work
He often gives us
But best of all is when
He lets me go home!

Hollie Evans (10)
St Columb Major Primary School, St Columb

THE SEASIDE!

The seaside,
Windy,
Silent
With only the waves splashing against the rocks.
The sand, full of shells and seaweed.
Seagulls flying round eating off the floor.
At summer
The summer sun glistens on the sea,
It stays out till late,
You could play all day and night.

Children screaming because they have to go home.
Barbecues being held in the summer holidays
With lamb and sausages and loads of other things.
I always argue with Mum because I don't want to go home!

Natasha Van Der Heiden (10)
St Columb Major Primary School, St Columb

MY SISTER

My sister is lucky to be alive,
But after a dreadful birth
She continued to strive.
A cheeky smile, a tantrum or two,
She was annoying but I loved her too.
Friends or enemies,
I cannot decide.
Sometimes I want to hide.
But what a boring time it would be
Without you near to me.

Siobhan Burt (8)
St Columb Major Primary School, St Columb

SEASONS

Spring is like a newborn life,
Shoots pushing their way through the soil,
Birds chirping in the trees,
Sweet young lambs being born,
Daffodils bobbing in the breeze.

Summer is the time to go to the beach,
And the weather is boiling hot.
Lots of visitors from different places,
The yellow sun shines a lot.

Autumn gets colder again.
Leaves fall off the trees in all different shades,
It's fun to jump in all the piles of leaves
And the light in the evening fades.

Winter is cold and frosty,
With snow you could make snowmen.
Cold fingers and nose,
Christmas is Jesus' birthday.
Sitting by the fire warming your toes.

Laura Cubeddu (9)
St Columb Major Primary School, St Columb

CATS

My two cats are called Harry and Tabitha,
They're really sweet.
They prowl around the house,
Tabitha the tiger pouncing upon each mouse
Harry is like a panther waiting for its prey.
My two cats, Harry and Tabitha.

Laura Pamplin (11)
St Columb Major Primary School, St Columb

THE POEM

I am going to write a poem,
I don't want it to rhyme.
I want it to be different,
But if not it wouldn't be a crime.
I'm going to write about . . .
I'm not sure of that yet,
I might write about my dog,
After all she is my pet.
I'll use adjectives and verbs,
I might use conjunctions.
But all the other nerds,
Will use time connectives.
I've suddenly realised,
What I'm doing with my time.
This piece that I have written,
Has turned into a rhyme!

Hayley Green (11)
St Columb Major Primary School, St Columb

MY BED

Tired and grumpy
But my bed's not lumpy
As I rest my weary head.
Bouncy and cosy
Making me dozy
That's how I describe my bed.

Charlotte Davidson (11)
St Columb Major Primary School, St Columb

MONTY

As white as snow,
As fluffy as a big ball of wool,
Always bobbing up and down,
Always playful.

Some time ago, he ran under the car,
What a terrible fright.
When we washed him, he splished and splashed,
There was more water on us than him.

One day he got lost,
We checked under the car in the hedges,
He was not there,
He'd run away.

I was upset,
I remembered when I was little
I pretended to be just like Monty!

Jenna Hobbs (9)
St Columb Major Primary School, St Columb

MY DREAM TRIP

My dream tip is to go to Scotland
Which is not a hot land,
I'd take all my friends with me,
And a happy time it shall be.

The best part is the Highlands,
The coldest place in the British Islands,
And in winter there is lots of snow,
Including rivers that will no longer flow.

For now I live on a farm,
Where all the chickens are safe from harm,
Although it is not quite fun,
I'm still waiting for my trip to be done.

Bethany Pamplin (8)
St Columb Major Primary School, St Columb

29

I had a very favourite cow
Her number 29.
She was a very pretty cow
I used to call her mine.

She had a short and stumpy tail
Her colour black and white
She used to moo and moo and moo
It gave me such delight.

The time passed by and then one day
My daddy said to me
'Your favourite cow has go to leave,
She's getting old you see.'

Six years I was with her
She sadly had to go
The vet came to take her away
But still I loved her so.

So 29 has gone away
And now I've got another
168 is now the best
Better than any other.

Sarah Colgrove (10)
St Columb Major Primary School, St Columb

PARTY ANIMAL

I'm a party animal that likes to groove,
I'm a party animal that likes to move,
I'm the party animal that always dances,
I'm the one that starts the prances.

I'm the one that takes all day,
To get ready for the end of the day,
I'm the one that likes to sing,
I'm the one that starts the swing.

Because,
I'm a party animal
I'm a party animal that likes to swing,
I'm a party animal that likes to bring . . .

A spice to all parties!

Kelsey Bartley (11)
St Columb Major Primary School, St Columb

MY PONY ROLO

My pony Rolo
He's a Dartmoor
He's brown around his nose and under the belly,
The rest of his body is black.
He's frisky,
Cute,
Funny
Sometimes naughty,
Loves children.
He's out on his own,
He's a lead rein pony . . .
I love him and he loves me!

Heidi Mercer (10)
St Columb Major Primary School, St Columb

JUNGLE

Sleeping lions in the midday sun,
Hairy hyenas having fun,
Monkeys swing from tree to tree,
Come on, let's go see!

Large animals, big and hairy,
Even little ones can be quite scary.
Elephants trunks swing from side to side,
I'm much too close, I'd better hide.
Trees stand still as can be,
Hope a monkey doesn't jump on me!

Benjamin Wearne (9)
St Columb Major Primary School, St Columb

MY DAD

My dad is like a roaring lion
when he is angry.
My dad is like a beautiful flower
when he is nice.
My dad is a hungry cheetah
when he is in a rush.
My dad likes watching football
when he is relaxing on the sofa.
Finally my dad is the best in the world -
when I want something.

Melissa Harvey (10)
St Columb Major Primary School, St Columb

MY GUINEA PIG

My guinea pig has big red eyes
Thick ginger coat
And short stumpy legs

She lives in a cage
With a nice bed of straw
She looks all cosy and warm

When I go to see her
She squeaks at me
She's very friendly
But all she does is *eat* and sleep

She eats lettuce and carrots
And bundles of hay
Cucumber and even stalks of broccoli
My guinea pig
Is the best guinea pig ever!

Sally Oram (11)
St Columb Major Primary School, St Columb

MY PETS

Happiness is having a pet,
Except when you have to take it to the vet,
When it's poorly it's not much fun,
But when it's well we can go for a run.

I have a cat and a hamster too,
Lots of animals live in a zoo,
In her wheel my hamster goes round,
The wheel squeaks and makes a crazy sound.

Emma Higgins (9)
St Columb Major Primary School, St Columb

THE CAT

Inside the cat's throat; the ominous siren.
Inside the ominous siren; the whirling colours.

Inside the cat's eyes; the enchanted moon.
Inside the enchanted moon; the sparkling treasure.

Inside the cat's pads; the luxurious cushion.
Inside the luxurious cushion; the comfort of the dawn.

Inside the cat's claw; the razor-sharp sickle.
Inside the razor-sharp sickle; the dark thunder clouds.

Inside the cat's fur; the white forest.
Inside the white forest; the swaying of the trees.

Inside the cat's tail; the rippling river.
Inside the rippling river; the nervous pebbles.

Holly Pearson (11)
St Giles-On-The-Heath Primary School, Launceston

FLOOD

Muddy, wet, soggy
Trees sinking into wet field
Sheep grey, dull,
Clouded.

Alex Bird (10)
St Giles-On-The-Heath Primary School, Launceston

THOUGHTS OF THE CAT

Inside the cat's throat; the broken glass
Inside the broken glass; the pain of his cry.

Inside the cat's eye; the roaring fire
Inside the roaring fire; the anger of his past.

Inside the cat's paw; a velvet cushion
Inside the velvet cushion; the luxury of his dreams.

Inside the cat's claw; the razor steel
Inside the razor steel; the isolation of his genius.

Inside the cat's tail; a whip of skin
Inside a whip of skin; the hatred of his soul.

Inside the cat's fur; the ripple of water
Inside the ripple of water; the confused and conscious friend.

Ben Hickey (11)
St Giles-On-The-Heath Primary School, Launceston

GOLDFISH

Hypnotic, swirling.
Mind blank.
Never wondering.
Forever the same.

Ben Davey (11)
St Giles-On-The-Heath Primary School, Launceston

122

DRAGON

Dragon exploded.
He snatched the fire from the blazing sun.
He stole the smoke from the burning wood
That made his fiery breath.
For his sharp pointed teeth,
He grabbed the shattered glass from the broken mirror.
He stole the whiteness from the moonlight.
His teeth were made.
For his scales,
He borrowed the wrinkled leaves from the ancient tree.
He captured the colour from the lime green grass
Which made his wrinkly scales.
For his wings,
He murdered the eagle for his huge wings.
He grasped the engine of a jet for its blistering speed.
Dragon landed.

Tanya Bishop & Naomi Elliott (10)
St Keverne Primary School, Helston

HAMSTER

Hamster appeared
He stole his eyes from the stars in the night sky
And that's how hamster got his eyes

He murdered the snake for his strong sharp teeth
And that's how hamster got his teeth

He seized the fur from the fluffy snow
And for his colour he snatched the tropical yellow sand
And that's how hamster was made

Joey Mitchell & Thomas Flockhart (9)
St Keverne Primary School, Helston

TIGER

Tiger developed
He stole the sharpness of the rocks,
He borrowed the colour of the tropical sands,
And the teeth were made.

He snatched the sharp glare from the snake,
He murdered the bleakness from the moor,
And the eyes appeared.

He took the coldness from the howling winds,
He grabbed the breeze from the clouds,
And the black nose formed.

He seized the lightning from a raging storm,
He demanded the blackness of the puma,
To make his fine coat.

He caught the hot bullet for his blistering speed.

He took the needles for his claws.

And tiger was completed.

Hannah Kueck (10) & Michelle Curnow (11)
St Keverne Primary School, Helston

HOW ADDER WAS MADE

Adder developed
He snatched his name from a sum
But lent it to a calculator
As long as he could still use it
He made his name

He grabbed his eyes from rubies
From the Queen's crown
He snatched his pattern
From a picture in an art gallery

124

He caught his skin from a fish
And the scales from a mermaid
And made his skin

He grabbed movement
From a worm as big as him
And made his tail

Sophie Pound & Emma Ladbrooke (10)
St Keverne Primary School, Helston

DOG COMMENCED

From the beach
He snatched the moisture from the sea slug
He snatched the slime from the seaweed
To create his nose.

From the forest
He borrowed the fur from the bear
He borrowed the pine needles from the fir tree
To form his coat and whiskers.

From the universe
He stole the sharpness from the spaceship
He stole the curve of the world
For his claws.

From Africa
He tackled the cheetah for his agility
He battled the lion for his strength
To construct his speed and muscles.

From the school he took the whiteness of the paper
He took the point of the pen for his teeth

And dog was complete.

Robert Carey & William Richards (11)
St Keverne Primary School, Helston

HOW TIGER WAS MADE

Tiger stole the black hearts of goblins to make his heart.

He stole the glitter from the stars and the light to make his eyes.

Tiger took the wings from the wind to make his blistering speed.

He took the snake's orange and black tail to make his own.

That is how tiger was made.

Emily Wood (11)
St Keverne Primary School, Helston

ANACONDA

Anaconda appeared.
He stole a 40-foot long rope to make his body and tail.

He grasped his hiss from the whistling wind.

To make his eyes and tongue
He robbed a chopstick and some cat's eyes.

Then anaconda was finished.

Ciar Lawson (9) & Daniel McPherson (10)
St Keverne Primary School, Helston

DOG APPEARED

He stole the tusks from a baby elephant,
He took the sharpness of a shark's fin to create his teeth.

He grabbed his tongue from a slippery snake,
He uses the movement of a cheetah when he is excited
To make his lick.

It took the motion of a windscreen wiper
To make the wagging of his tail.
He took the howling of the wind
To make his bark.

Stephanie Pearce (10) & Holly Nicholls (11)
St Keverne Primary School, Helston

RAT APPEARED

He took the teeth from the grass snake
He took the speed from the athlete
He took the squeak from the mouse
He took the feet from the hamster
For his tail he took the worm from the ground
To make his eyes he took the beads from a child's purse
For his claws he took the shattered glass
Rat appeared.

Jake Denman (10)
St Keverne Primary School, Helston

THE OCTOPUS

It stole the pink from a coral reef,
And snatched olives from trees for its eyes,
Seaweed stuck with tar for legs,
The moon's craters were pinched for clinging.

Its costume of rubber was made from tyres,
Its head was made from glittering steel,
The white in its eyes was made from the stars.

Swimming from coast to coast like the wind in a sail,
This is the octopus.

Caroline Hawkins (11), Tammy White (10) & Tammy Retallack (9)
St Keverne Primary School, Helston

DOG APPEARED

Dog started
She murdered a crow to make her angry bark
She shook a frog for her threatening growl
So her voice was made

For her coat
She stole from a sheep to get her rough fur
She snatched the golden sand
So her coat was made

For her run
She grabbed the threatening wind
She pulled the speed out of the cheetah
So her run was made

She took the body of a moose
She caught the legs of a camel
So her body was made

For her eyes
She stole the stars from the deep blue sky
She nicked the darkness of the night sky

Melanie Clayton & Kaylee Spooner (10)
St Keverne Primary School, Helston

BEAR BEGAN

The creation of the bear commenced
He stole the roar of the lion
He murdered the dog for its growl
That made bear's voice.

For his claws
He stole the sharpness of a sword
He took the crescent moon
And his claws appeared.

For some teeth
He took the sharpness of a knife
And the whiteness of paper
And he had his teeth.

For his fur he stole the brownness of the tree trunk
He took the softness of the snow
And his fur appeared
And bear was complete.

Toby Trimble & James Richards (10)
St Keverne Primary School, Helston

LION

Lion crept,
He snatched the brightness of the moonlight,
And the blackness of the night sky,
And made his sparkly eyes.

He crept around the forest, breaking twigs as he moved his heavy feet,
And made his prowl from a tornado.

He snatched the claws from an eagle,
The white of the newly-fallen snow,
And made his shining white teeth.

He snatched the roar of thunder,
And the rumble of the volcano,
And made his roar.

Tania Harris & Sarah Harris (10)
St Keverne Primary School, Helston

MOUSE WAS MADE

Mouse was made by stealing shadowy beads as eyes from my mother's
    jewellery box

Then under the ground she stole the worm for her flickering long tail

She murdered the gerbil for her snuffly nose

She took the softness of the snow for her silky fur

And flinched the whiskers of the cat to have as her own

She killed the eagle for its claws to make her paws as hot as fire

And mouse was finally born!

Sally Hewett & Kathy Macfarlane (9)
St Keverne Primary School, Helston

WORMS ARMAGEDDON

We are now entering the Worms Armageddon computer game.

W orms are the champions of war.
O ther bugs don't stand a chance.
R emember who's the boss.
M embers of the public should fear them.
S heep will explode and protect the base.

R uins of the battlefield, black and destroyed.
U ullimited bombs help the soldiers blast their enemy
L ove does not exist in this tribe.
E nding of the war is unknown.
S witching off the computer now.

David Quinn (10)
St Kew Primary School, Bodmin

THE OGRE

There once lived a terrible ogre
Who always wore a toga,
He was very big and fat
And he had a tiger for a cat.
He lived in a cave,
But he wasn't very brave,
And one stormy night he got scared,
The problem was that no one cared.
He ran outside and started to cry,
Then he shouted,
'No one cares if I live or die.'
Then a man came, he said,
'You can sleep in my house,
I have a spare bed.'

PS. The moral to this poem is, not everyone hates ogres.

Christopher Scott (10)
St Kew Primary School, Bodmin

SPRING POEM

Singing birds flying in the morning sun.
Playing lambs with woolly coats.
Ringing snowdrops with gentle stems.
Interesting blossom on the trees.
Nothing stirring but a gentle breeze.
Green spring grass for the animals to enjoy.

Edward Harris (11)
St Kew Primary School, Bodmin

IMAGINE

Imagine a slug as big as a rug,
Imagine a rat as big as a cat,
Imagine a cake as long as a rake,
Imagine a hen as long as a pen,
Imagine a nit as big as a pit,
Imagine a tree as small as my knee,
Imagine a knight as small as a light,
Imagine me the size of a flea,
Imagine a toy as big as a boy,
Imagine a wall the size of a ball,
Imagine a hole as long as a pole,
Imagine a whale as small as a nail,
Imagine a tramp the size of a lamp.

Donna Allen (10)
St Kew Primary School, Bodmin

SNAKE IN THE GRASS

Slithering sliding snakes
Slither through the grass
Sliding like a rake
Trying to win a race
Wanting to eat a cake
Making an easy escape
But winning all day
And never wanting to go away

Lewis Scott (11)
St Kew Primary School, Bodmin

WORMS

Entering Worms CD

W ild worms are back ready for war
O ther teams don't stand a chance
R emember who's the boss
M embers of staff blow up houses
S uper sheep will make you fly away

W orld war worms
O h yes there was definitely contact there
R uins of the battlefield
L umpy custard rule
D irections to kill

P eople must fear
A rmageddon is near
R eady to rumble
T raitor
Y eah, we won
S witching off computer, worms destroyed

Mark Oakes (10)
St Kew Primary School, Bodmin

AT THE BEACH

As I walked down the steps onto the beach
I saw the waves crashing on the rocks
The seagulls looking for food
I saw little children playing in the sand
The fish swimming in the shallow waters
I saw water running down the rocks
The water sparkling in the rock pools

Ben Dufort (11)
St Kew Primary School, Bodmin

RESCUE AT SEA

R   avaging waves engulfing the sea,
E   choing calls of the rescuers,
S   limy cliffs making it harder to hang on,
C   alling still rapid, blocked by the wind,
U   seful ropes get washed away,
E   choing of calls getting louder.

A   ching arms trying to hold on.
T   railers and rescue vehicles closing in.

S   lipping of the hands,
E   mitting calls, person rescued!
A   nything could happen at sea!

David Kenneth Blake (11)
St Kew Primary School, Bodmin

SHARKS

Swimming sharks round and round
Having a good time searching the ground
A whale fish swims away,
Round the corner a shark spots it prey,
Killing people, sealife as well
Sound the alarm, it's like a bell!

Friendly fishes swim to you,
Interesting seaweed coming through,
Silly crabs fighting,
Huge lobsters biting.

Amelia Louise Bonel (10)
St Kew Primary School, Bodmin

ON THE BEACH

On the beach I see,
The custard sand
And the potion sea,
Shoals of silver fish,
Seaweed waving its green locks,
Mysterious creatures drifting out to sea,
Cries of the seagull,
As the sun slips under the beach.

Gosel Tom-Baird (11)
St Kew Primary School, Bodmin

THE SINGING COCK

The singing cock,
Makes the seagulls rock,
And the cows are milking in tune.

The horses are prancing,
And the pigs are dancing,
He makes the chickens dance to the moon.

The sheep are movers,
And the peacocks are groovers,
And he could keep on going all night.

The farmer doesn't like him any more,
So he ate an apple core,
And that was the end of him.

Hannah Gill (8)
St Mabyn CE Primary School, Bodmin

COOKING

Rice and curry,
Cream and jelly,
Pans and pots,
I want *lots!*
Yummy, scrumptious food!

Sizzling, roasted,
Baked, toasted,
Pancake in a pan,
Buns on a plate,
Food is me mate.

A bowl of ice cream,
I dreamt it in my dream,
Cream cakes,
Delicious steaks,
I like them and no mistakes.

Emilie Penfold (9)
St Mabyn CE Primary School, Bodmin

TEDDY BEAR

My teddy bear is soft,
My teddy bear is khaki,
I love my dear teddy bear.
My teddy bear is warm and has a pink nose,
My teddy bear is happy,
I love my dear teddy bear.
My teddy bear is pretty,
My teddy bear is a prize bear,
I love my dear teddy bear.

Samantha Edwards (8)
St Mabyn CE Primary School, Bodmin

HAUNTED HOUSE

Down to the haunted house they go
Being so quiet as they know,
The ghosts of St Mabyn come out at night
Then back home at one o'clock and out of sight.
Over the green grass hill they go
Being so quiet as they know,
If they come out at day
We will find their secret pathway.
One o'clock, one o'clock, be in bed
Or else they will take your soul,
The police will be careful
And hide when they arrive.
Over the green grass hill they go,
Being so quiet as they know.

Bryony Buckland (10)
St Mabyn CE Primary School, Bodmin

TIGGER

Tigger is springy and bouncy too
He always bounces on top of Pooh
He's never bored, he's got lots of friends
Piglet, Pooh, Rabbit, Owl, not forgetting Roo
Whenever he's sad and all alone
He goes to find Piglet and Pooh and Roo
He's stripy and bouncy and has lots of fun
Because he's the only one.

Jacelyn Hawkey (8)
St Mabyn CE Primary School, Bodmin

SNAKES

Snakes are slimy,
Long and scary.
Snakes are deadly,
Slippery and shiny.

Snakes can kill you,
Eat you and swallow you!
If you saw a snake,
You would probably run a mile!

Snakes are poisonous,
Long and stretchy,
Snakes are greedy,
Slippery and smooth.

But they don't scare me!

Hollie Runnalls (9)
St Mabyn CE Primary School, Bodmin

TARANTULA

Tarantulas are beastly,
Bony and big,
Fast and really hard.

They're hairy, bushy,
Tough too, big, furious,
Messy with spiky hair.

Tarantulas have razor-sharp teeth,
Tarantulas just want to kill,
Well that's what people think!

They're camouflaged too,
They can be big or small,
But there's something you don't want to do -
Don't mess with a tarantula.

Robbie Jones (10)
St Mabyn CE Primary School, Bodmin

A HAUNTED HOUSE

A haunted house is dangerous,
Frightful and smelly.

A haunted house is misty,
Muddy, murky.

A haunted house is monstrous,
You just don't know what to do!

A haunted house is empty,
Waiting for you to pop into.

A haunted house is scary,
Don't go in there
It will swallow you or something
Or give you nightmares!

Rebecca Blake (9)
St Mabyn CE Primary School, Bodmin

THE OLD FOREST

The Old Forest has old oak trees,
They have grown as far as you can see,
The animals live peacefully in harmony.

The badgers, rabbits, insects and deer,
All live in no fear.

In the spring there are many flowers,
The trees get back their leaves and look like towers.

In the summer the sun peeps through,
Twigs crack and crumble too.

In the autumn there are mounds of leaves,
Any colour from any tree.

In the winter the trees are bare,
They all stand together pair by pair.

The Old Forest has old oak trees.

Katie Welch (10)
St Mabyn CE Primary School, Bodmin

SCHOOL

Some like school, some do not
And if you don't here is the plot.
Sneak in there in the middle of the night
And destroy everything that comes to your sight.

Maths, English, science too,
Destroy everything, it's good for you!
Teachers come in and yell out loud,
'How dare you do this, your brain's like a cloud!'

Finally when out of trouble,
(The teachers are tidying up the rubble.)
I've been expelled, oh yes! Yippee!
I told you it would work, see?

Harriet Smith (10)
St Mabyn CE Primary School, Bodmin

THE WHITE HORSE

As the horse jumps the waves
With its waving mane,
Her name is Sea and Sun
And she has a lot of fun.
Then she sees some lightning
That is very frightening.
She hunts a log
And jumps at a frog,
So you can see my force
Upon a white horse.

Sophie Gaskell (10)
St Mabyn CE Primary School, Bodmin

A RAINBOW

A rainbow will shine and glisten and gleam.
A rainbow is colourful, beautiful and bright.
A rainbow is multicoloured.
A rainbow is amazing, golden and sparkling.
A rainbow is a miracle.

Jessica Cox (8)
St Mabyn CE Primary School, Bodmin

THE STORM!

A storm is coming
The wind is humming
Like an angry, buzzing bee
The yellow shining lightning
That is frightening
The trees are waving
The waves are rushing
The clouds are pushing
A storm is coming.

Tammy Ash (10)
St Mabyn CE Primary School, Bodmin

BEACH DAYS

The sea is singing,
When the sun comes up.
Beautiful waves crash on the surf,
People on the sand
Sleeping, sunbathing, surfing.
Children playing happily.
Digging huge holes.
Collecting special shells fro sandcastles.
Sometimes a whale's washed up on a beach.
Stuck!
Waiting for those crashing clashing waves to hit the shore.
When it's time to go
You can see sand slipping off the rocks
Going drip, drop, drip, drop, drip.

Becky Nobes (10)
St Mewan Primary School, St Austell

A PERFECT BEACH

Dancing dolphins dive in delight,
The sky looks like fire, but it's only the sunset,
Fish party as if it's a disco,
White horses happily trot along the sandy beach.

The beach is left without any shells,
Sea-water is soft, gentle and calm,
A soft breeze blows sand into the sea,
Eels climb slowly, smiling softly.

Shells have been collected,
Swift and smooth the tide comes in,
The boats glide away,
Surfers slowly swimming safely to the shore.

Deep dark blue water washes up,
The moon reflects on the water,
As if it's saying 'Hello' to its partner.

Seagulls screeches slowly, silently dying,
Boats are tied up as if they're dangerous,
The wildlife has disappeared, all is quiet,
Midnight and everybody has gone.

Claire Sweet (9)
St Mewan Primary School, St Austell

MURDER

Murder is the colour of black,
It smells like treachery.
It sounds like a lamb at the slaughter
And feels like a creature too gross to describe.
It lives in evil people's souls.

Tom Arjomandi (10)
St Mewan Primary School, St Austell

MY DREAM BEACH

Dolphins diving deep down in delight,
Sharks showing off their sharp teeth,
Fish that look like they've eaten too much Christmas pudding,
Crabs crawling up craggy rocks crazily.

Sunken ships once sailed softly and slowly,
People pacing peacefully, plodding along perfectly,
The sun so bright it looks like a lit-up flare,
Bubbling bright buffalo fish with bulging brains.

White whales wildly whizzing through the water,
Waves whooshing wildly,
Mad monkfish,
Boats that look like bananas.

Wildlife wickedly wading through the water,
Children eating everything in sight,
Dogs digging down, down, down in the sand,
Fish so colourful, like a parrot.
Black and white horses stream across the line of the sea,
Galloping all of the way,
Looking like a flash of lightning,
It sounds like a thunderstorm fading into the distance.

Joanne Dyer (9)
St Mewan Primary School, St Austell

HEAT

H   anging Around In Tropical Places,
E   quator Is Getting Hot,
A   mazon River Flowing Gently,
T   emperature Rising Across The World.

Caroline Swain (10)
St Mewan Primary School, St Austell

WAR

War is the colour of brown, black and red merged into one.
It smells like a Tudor hospital.
It tastes of 'Fisherman's Friend' tablets.
It sounds like sweetcorn popping.
It feels angry yet terrified.
It lives in stubborn minds.

Anna Robinson (10)
St Mewan Primary School, St Austell

CONFIDENCE

Confidence is the colour of blue
It smells bold and bright
It tastes of achievement
It sounds like a clapping crowd
It feels congratulating
It lives in your courage.

Hollie Abbott (10)
St Mewan Primary School, St Austell

PAIN

Pain is the colour of a rainbow set in stone
It smells like a rat-infested sewer
It tastes like grit and tears from the heart
It sounds like a murder victim's last cries of 'help'!
It feels like freezing water rising in your chest
It lives in the coffin of life
Just waiting to be dug up and used again.

Ellie Beer (10)
St Mewan Primary School, St Austell

STORMY DAY

Splish splosh goes the sea
As it roars like a tiger
The sea goes wild as tremendous, terrifying thunder strikes the land
Forked lightning lights up the whole beach
Everything goes silent for a while
A *big* wave hits the land
The sea goes wild once more
A *huge* strike of thunder
All the people run from the beach really fast
Lunches flying everywhere
After the storm all is still;
One last lash of lightning
As frightened as a dog in distress
The people creep back to the terrifying terrible yet tremendous beach.

Claire Bassett (9)
St Mewan Primary School, St Austell

SEA SONG

The sea is singing, across the horizon
Orange, red, yellow, purple
Like a colourful rainbow
Dolphins jumping through the waves
Their skin as shiny as the sun
People sunbathing
Their skin as red as a rose
Reading books
Children playing happily
Making huge sandcastles
Collecting shiny shells and perfect pebbles
To take back to school
Ice creams and ice lollies dripping slowly onto the sand.

Julie Thompson (9)
St Mewan Primary School, St Austell

MY IMAGINARY BEACH

Quiet, calm, relaxing sounds,
Sea lapping at the soft, sandy shore.
Seagulls squawking, searching,
The soft sand tickles my toes.

Deep rock pools shimmer and shine,
Crabs creeping slowly around,
Footprints are blown away
In the salty sea breeze.

Boats swaying on the horizon,
A calm, flat sea.
Driftwood drifts onto the shore,
Sun rays beat down.

This beach is mine,
And always will be,
Deserted it will stay,
For now and evermore.

Emma Clayton (10)
St Mewan Primary School, St Austell

THE SEA

The sea is crashing like wind wailing away.
The wind is whistling in a nasty voice.
The sun comes out and dolphins are joking
And jumping under a rainbow shining brightly.
Dogs darting away from big waves.
People play playfully in the soft sand.
Crabs being captured and put into buckets.
Waterfalls whooshing wildly.

Kelsey Greenaway (10)
St Mewan Primary School, St Austell

THE GENTLE SEA

The sea is as gentle as a whale
Waves frothy and smooth
Starfish floating on the top waiting
Dolphins jumping silently
Whales swimming and searching for food
Swinging, swaying, softly shimmering sea
Singing sea whistling and wailing

F r e e

Flying seagulls snatch fish
Scavenging delicious starfish
What a place. . .

Nicola Merrifield (9)
St Mewan Primary School, St Austell

SEASIDE COOL!

Soft, squidgy sand,
Wet, wild waves,
Lovely ladies lick lollies.
Beach babes bounce balls.
Cans of beer popped open.
Dolphins diving,
Surf shacks,
Just surviving!
Small rivers stretch to the sea.
Seals swimming.
Dogs digging.
What a way to be!

Jenny Bee (9)
St Mewan Primary School, St Austell

A WORLD OF WATER

The wailing water waves go freely,
Children climbing high on rocks,
Seagulls' songs sound sweet
As they dive for food
Sand is wet where the sea has been
Feet sinking slowly
Water blue and very warm
Swimmers splashing
Sandcastles in-between sunbathers
Seaweed and stones stick in shallow water
Deep water is dark, dark green
Crawling crabs try to hide.

Ben Barnes (9)
St Mewan Primary School, St Austell

THE SEA

The crushing sea pushes up against the rocks,
Like a fierce lion hunting for its dinner.
Different coloured fish swimming,
Swifting, swaying, softly moving.
Seaweed swirling in the wind.
Dolphins jumping over waves,
Tails and fins splashing.
Sailors, sail silently.
Sharks disguising themselves,
Trying to catch their dinner.
The sun is a shining ball of fire.
Its brightness reflecting onto the sea.

Karla Tellam (10)
St Mewan Primary School, St Austell

PEACE

Peace is the colour of white
It smells like Heaven
It tastes like green fields
It sounds like ladies singing
It feels like a butterfly
It lives in Heaven.

Richard Hill (10)
St Mewan Primary School, St Austell

PAIN

Black is the colour of pain
It smells like hot car wheels
It tastes of fire and smoke
It sounds like somebody dying
It feels like the end of the world
It lives in the undergrowth.

Alastair Hendry (9)
St Mewan Primary School, St Austell

PEACE

Peace is the colour of purple.
It smells of roses
It tastes like thin air.
It sounds like a river flowing.
It feels like dancing.
It lives in me!

Kelly Martin (10)
St Mewan Primary School, St Austell

JEALOUSY

Jealousy is the colour of dark green
It smells like hot raging steam spouting from a teapot
It tastes like a wobbly jelly wobbling jealously
It sounds like a stormy sea, crashing against rocks whirling fearlessly
It feels like your hands are clenching together
It lives in your very own mind.

Sarah Newing (9)
St Mewan Primary School, St Austell

HEAVEN

Heaven is the colour of white.
It smells like strawberries.
It tastes like wine.
It sounds so sweet.
It feels like you're floating to the stars.
It lives in the clouds.

Lewis Bishop (9)
St Mewan Primary School, St Austell

MISERY

Misery is the colour of hot tea
It smells like mouldy beer
It tastes like a hundred pounds down the drain
It sounds like a drum beating so hard against your body
It feels like a volcano bubbling lava
It lives in my head where its friends are

Adam Brenton (9)
St Mewan Primary School, St Austell

A DAY AT THE BEACH

Waves crashing on the rocks
People sunbathing
On the sand.

Boats bobbing on the water
People crabbing
On the side.

Men fishing in the ocean
Fish swimming
Down below.

Sea gulls squabbling for food
People eating their lunches.

People skimming stones
In the water
Children playing in the sand.

Crabs crawling creepily
Octopus using their suckers
Sharks swimming swiftly.

Ben Beynon (9)
St Mewan Primary School, St Austell

FRIENDSHIP

Friendship is the colour of yellow,
It smells like roses,
It tastes of happiness,
It sounds like summer coming,
It feels like you're in a dream,
It lives in my heart.

Kelly Swiggs (9)
St Mewan Primary School, St Austell

THE NETBALL MATCH

When we arrived at Penryn,
I was jumping for joy in my knees,
I felt like I was made of tin,
Suddenly I was holding some keys.

I started to feel sour,
So mum gave me a drink,
But that gave me more power,
And that made me think.

Then the match began,
I felt like an elastic band,
And if I was, I was about to go twang,
Then I started to land.

Then they scored
But we couldn't
We didn't get bored
Give up? We wouldn't?

Then it happened again,
But we didn't fret,
We knew we could retain,
2 goals, you bet!

The full time whistle went,
Then we had a chat,
The umpire said, 'Well done, girls,'
And we were proud of that.

Laura Steadman (11)
St Mewan Primary School, St Austell

UNDERWATER

Dolphins are dancing in delight
Stingrays swim silently I the sea
Sharks creep around the open water
Octopus opens his squishy legs
Fish scared to death by the sharks
Shells being broken by fierce creatures
Water dark, dark green
Starfish nowhere to be seen

Craig Smith (9)
St Mewan Primary School, St Austell

PAIN

Pain is the colour of blue
It smells like hot burning oil
It tastes like metal
It sounds like a lion roaring
It feels like someone's screaming
It lives in our mind

Michael Berry (9)
St Mewan Primary School, St Austell

DEATH

Death is the colour of crimson
It smells of an old house
It tastes of boiled cabbage
It sounds of heavy metal
It feels like a quivering heart
It lives in old age and carelessness

Nathan Price (9)
St Mewan Primary School, St Austell

THE MYSTERIOUS LAKE

The trees stand tall, around the lake
Like dark, dingy dungeons
Water lapping against the island
Like the breeze of summer
Fish swimming silently away
Like a coloured rainbow hovering near the bottom
People canoeing in their Wendab canoe
Waves hit my feet
Making a gentle splash
Feeling the breeze of the pink, purple, orange sunset.

Emma Ead (9)
St Mewan Primary School, St Austell

OCEAN LIFE

In the ocean,
I see darting, diving, dancing dolphins.
Sharks teeth as sharp as knives.
Octopus with sticky suckers.
Fishes fins, flapping as fast as a rocket shooting through space.
Lobsters crawling along the ocean floor.
Fish hiding in coral, away from sharks.
Stingrays disguising themselves.
Jellyfish floating fearlessly.
Swishing, swaying seaweed streams by
Waving at all the creatures in the ocean.

Jack Watterson (9)
St Mewan Primary School, St Austell

SPLASH OF WATER

Gigantic waves lashing,
Up and down,
On the dirty, dark, dislocated rock.
Smacking smartly into smithereens.
Seagulls soaring, shouting, shooting through the air.
Raindrops turning into awful, anxious hail.
Falling from the heavenly cloud, foggy and grey.
Sea as rough as a volcano.

Alex Harwood (10)
St Mewan Primary School, St Austell

HATE

Hate is the colour of black,
It smells like used tissue,
It tastes of petrol
It sounds like thunder
It feels like stone,
It lives in my stomach.

Matthew Johnstone (9)
St Mewan Primary School, St Austell

MY DREAM

I want to be a superstar,
Hopefully I will go far.
I really want to write a song,
That people sing all day long!

I want to be on TV shows,
So people say, 'There she goes.'
I want to go to very hot places,
I want to see smiles on children's faces.

I want to be welcomed into shops,
I want to be asked on Top of the Pops.
I want to have my own CD,
I want to make a DVD.

I want to meet S Club 7,
If this is real then I'm in Heaven.
I want to be given strawberries and cream,
I want people to know this is my dream!

Raegan Metters (11)
St Mewan Primary School, St Austell

UNDERWATER

The water is like a crystal ball,
Underwater fish are shining flames of hot fire.
Fish meet their doom with sharks,
Sharks are dingy, dark and deadly.
Divers attack sharks.
Fish hide behind colourful rocks.
Underwater is a dangerous place.
At night sharks appear to find their prey.

Michael Williams (9)
St Mewan Primary School, St Austell

DEATH

Death is the colour of red
It smells like a smoky fire
It tastes of sick
It sounds like a violent thunderstorm
It feels like fire
It lives in your spirit

Antony Baron (9)
St Mewan Primary School, St Austell

SUNSHINE

Sunshine is a glistening river,
Sparkling like a golden ring.
It gives us glowing harvest,
Spreading joy over the world.
As the sunflowers open in the morning,
So the sunshine opens my heart.
Sunshine is a sandy beach,
Spreading its glory everywhere.
Sunshine is a pot of gold,
That's big enough for everyone.
Bright, glistening, sparkling, friendly,
This for me is sunshine.

Emily Waterhouse (10)
St Petrocs School, Bude

SUNSHINE

Sunshine is a vanilla ice cream,
Dripping like bright yellow paint.
It keeps the world happy,
And puts smiles on our faces.
As the corn sways,
The sun turns it gold.
Sunshine is a sandy beach,
Surrounded by a blue wave.
Sunshine is a pot of gold,
Like the end of a beautiful rainbow.
Bright, happy, friendly, fire,
This for me is sunshine.

Sally Biddlecombe (11)
St Petrocs School, Bude

IN THE WOODS

Acorns, hard to crack
Old earthy woods
Splashing, gurgling river
Fungi on old trees
Boots snapping twigs
Birds flying high over the woods
Nettles sting
Pigeons cooing
Trees sway from side to side
Smooth, spiky holly
Chestnuts so prickly
Ivy climbing trees
Brown leaves so crisp
Birds swoop down on beetles
Larch leaves so delicate
Beetles scuffling

Oliver Dell (8)
St Petrocs School, Bude

A TEMPERATURE POEM

At zero, I shivered like some jelly.
At 5°c, I was as cold as ice.
At 10°c, I was as cool as new water.
At 15°c, I was as mild as a spring day.
At 20°c, I was as warm as a pizza.
At 25°c, I was as hot as a volcano.
At 35°c, I was as sweltering as the sun.

Edward Northen (8)
St Petrocs School, Bude

A TEMPERATURE POEM

At zero, I shivered like jelly.
At 5°c, I was as cold as ice.
At 10°c, I was as cool as a breeze.
At 15°c, I was as mild as a bed.
At 20°c, I was as warm as a fire.
At 25°-30°c, I was as hot as a summer day.
At 35°c, I was sweltering like the sun.

Rebekah Locke (8)
St Petrocs School, Bude

I AM THE SAME

I can smell
I can see
I can touch
I can taste
I can hear

    I am the same
    I am the same

I can smell the burning of the air
I can see the waves in the sea
I can touch the ice upon my fingers
I can taste the frog in my throat as it jumps
I can hear you as you speak

    I am the same
    I am the same

I am black, you are white
I can still be the same

Karly Phillips (10)
St Stephen Churchtown Primary School, St Austell

I'M THE SAME

I'm the same
I'm the same

I can smell the chicken in the oven
You can too

I'm the same
I'm the same

I can see the stars at night
You can too

I'm the same
I'm the same

I can touch a thousand things
You can too

I'm the same
I'm the same

I can taste a lot of different food
You can too

I'm the same
I'm the same

I can hear the waves crash against the rocks
You can too

I'm the same
I'm the same

Victoria Newman (10)
St Stephen Churchtown Primary School, St Austell

DISABILITY

D on't offend the disabled
I   f I'm disabled, it doesn't matter
S top and think
A nyone could help
B e kind
I   t's the inside that counts
L ooks are nothing, thoughts are
I   t's not the colour that matters
T hink of others
Y ou're no different

Jessie Cleverley (10)
St Stephen Churchtown Primary School, St Austell

WAR

War is red,
It smells like smoke of guns;
It tastes like dark soil.
War sounds like bombs exploding.
It feels like a million knives stabbing at once.

Jon-Pierre Oleszynski (9)
St Stephen Churchtown Primary School, St Austell

PLAYING WITH FRIENDS!

Friends playing,
   Friends singing,
      Friends drawing,
         Friends swimming,
         Friends painting.

Friends working,
   Friends chatting,
      Friends shouting,
         Friends running!

Hayley Gregory (8)
St Stephen's Primary School, Launceston

IN MY HEART I CARRY

In my heart I carry
All the fantastic excellent fun times
I had with my grandad.

In my heart I carry
All the hot, cold, fun trips
I went on with my gran.

In my heart I carry
All the love and holidays
I have gone on with my mum and dad.

In my heart I carry
All the times Aaron and Darren, my brothers
Have beaten me up.

In my heart I carry
All my friends, Zoe, Jade, Charlotte, Jodie
For being there for me.

In my heart I carry
All the teachers
For always helping me with my work.

In my heart I carry
Everyone for always doing our own things.

Kayleigh Trewin (10)
St Stephen's Primary School, Launceston

PLAYING FOOTBALL

Football flying
Mud splattering
People slipping
Opposition falling
Everyone shouting
Big people squashing
Little people slipping
Home team winning

David Spence (8)
St Stephen's Primary School, Launceston

WATER FUN

Children splashing,
Babies crying,
Mothers shouting,
Toddlers drowning,
Water flowing,
People bouncing,
Adults diving,
Fathers lazing,
They've gone all crazy!

Sophie Duke (8)
St Stephen's Primary School, Launceston

SLIPPERY SNAKES

Some snakes slip, slide and slither
Some snakes slither, slip and slide.

Some frogs flip, flap and flop
Some frogs flop, flip and flap.

Some lions leap, lie and lick
Some lions lick, leap and lie.

Some tarantulas tickle, tremble and terrify
Some tarantulas terrify, tickle and tremble.

Rachael Spittle (10)
St Stephen's Primary School, Launceston

SWIMMING WITH DOLPHINS

Smoothly swimming
Dolphins squealing
Children playing
Adults wheeling
Toddlers drowning
People shouting
Grandad fishing
Granny chatting
Mum and dad swimming

Jazmin Dummer (8)
St Stephen's Primary School, Launceston

ICE!

Strolling down Zulu lane,
Crunching, crackling, crispy-white.
Slipping on frosty ice,
Skidding, sliding, head over heels.
Bouncing down cold steps,
Bomb, bang, crack,
Sore back! Oh, oh, oh,
Ouch!

Christopher Parnell (9)
St Stephen's Primary School, Launceston

SLIMY BOOTS

Up the rocky muddy mountain
Squelching, splashing, squeaking
One foot deep in slimy mud
Smashing, bopping, clashing

Halfway up the slimy mountain
Squeaky, splashy, crackly
One foot high in rocky mud
Splashy, sploshy, squeaky

At the top of the mountain
Bang, smash, crash
One foot deep in slimy mud
Squelch, splosh, squeak

Coming down the mountain
Crash, bang, wallop
One foot deep in rocky mud
Smash, bang, crash

At the foot of the mountain
Smash, wallop, bop
One foot high in slimy mud
Trickling, throdging, banging

In a field
Squeaky, splashy, trickly
Two foot deep in watery mud
Splashing, sploshing, trickling

On the hard rocky road
Bang, crash, wallop
One inch deep in slimy mud
Wallop, squeak, squelch

Davinia Vincent (10)
St Stephen's Primary School, Launceston

MY EMPTY BELLY

In my empty belly
There is nothing
I hear it rumbling
I hear it squelching at me
'Give me some food,' it squelched.

In my empty belly
There is nothing
Soon it's going to burst with growls
'Grrr, ssss,' it's shouting.

'Bam, give me some food.'

The door bell goes ding dong
It's mum, she's got some food
She pours me the crackling Frosties
One mouthful whizzes down my throat
It's happy now.

It's morning again!
Hang on, something's happening
My tummy starts rumbling again, *oh no!*
'Gree,' it goes again, 'I need some food quick.'
I run downstairs and trash the cupboards
Bang, wallop
All there is is sauce, chocolate spread and things like that.
I look through the cereal cupboards
Nothing
'Mum, Mum,' I shout, 'Where's cereal?'
She isn't in
Hang on
There's a knock at the door
Is it mum?
I wonder . . .

Ellie Hardy (10)
St Stephen's Primary School, Launceston

I See On The Way To The Sea

I am walking on the beach
Splish, splash, wash
I see crabs on the way
Rustle, ristle, rash

I walk in a rock pool
Sploosh, splosh, wham
I see a fish
Swishle, swashle, swash

I splash in the sea
Whish, whirl, splot
I see a starfish
Silent, creepy
Splish, splosh, splash
It disappears
It's home time for us both!

Ashley Cooper (9)
St Stephen's Primary School, Launceston

A Forest Winter Walk

Wellington boots crunching in the snow,
Crispy, prispy, brispy, wispy.
We leave footprints on our journey,
Quively, curvy, swively, swivy.

Along go the forest travellers,
Clomp, blomp, dlomp, flomp.
One of the travellers stepped on a twig,
Click, snick, crick, *snap!*

The forest travellers gather up the twigs and leaves,
Rustle, hustle, tustle, bustle.
They make a golden fire,
Hackle, crackle, snackle, fackle.

Zoë Prosser (10)
St Stephen's Primary School, Launceston

PLAYING IN THE WATER

People splashing
    Water flying
Babies drowning
    Mothers shouting
Children fighting
    Toddlers crying
Feet splashing
    Children leaving.

Elliot Hancock (9)
St Stephen's Primary School, Launceston

PLAYING IN WATER

People splashing,
    Children screaming,
        Parents relaxing,
            Pets drowning,
                Teachers sleeping,
                    Babies crying,
                        Toddlers slipping.

Kelly Chapman (8)
St Stephen's Primary School, Launceston

IN THE MORNING

In the morning the alarm goes off,
Bring, ting, aling,
Downstairs I run, bang, dong, ding,
Sit down for breakfast and hear the kettle boiling,
Boil, gurgle, whistle,
Hear the toasting popping,
Pop, ping, cackling.

In the morning I hear the taps running,
Splash, splish, splosh,
Telly speaking,
Speak, speak, speak.

In the morning I hear dogs barking,
Bark, howl, bark,
Cat purring,
Purr, purr, purr,
Rabbit sniffing,
Sniffle, sniffle, sniffle.

That's what happens in my morning.

Jodie Hannah Karen O'Neill (10)
St Stephen's Primary School, Launceston

BEACH

The sun shone down on the slodely sand,
The purple tried to get a tan.
Sandy shoes, sposhingly lay nearby,
The seagulls making children cry.

The waves beating sloppily against the rocks,
Ptompf, the waves sloshed,
Caboom, into the wall,
Capooth, as they were so tall.

The day comes to a whirling end
The beach will be quiet again,
The sand is stodgy and wet
The waves settle and set.

Nakita Houghton (9)
St Stephen's Primary School, Launceston

GOING HOME

Children running
Children dashing
Children racing
Children rushing
Children hurrying
Children jogging
Children sprinting
Children zooming
Children speeding
Going home!

Nathan Parsons (9)
St Stephen's Primary School, Launceston

COMING TO SCHOOL

Coats dragging,
Hearts thumping,
Feet pacing,
Mothers yelling,
Cars zooming,
Children moaning,
Children dawdling,
Babies crying,
Children leaving.

Nikki Cornelius (9)
St Stephen's Primary School, Launceston

MORNING COMES

Morning comes with mums yelling.
Morning comes with toast popping.
Morning comes with kettles singing.
Morning comes with people having showers.
Morning comes with toilets flushing.
Morning comes with cars moving.
Morning comes with cats miaowing and dogs barking.
Morning comes with phones ringing.
Morning comes with doors banging.
Morning comes with birds tweeting.
Morning comes with sun rising.
Morning comes with clocks ticking.
Morning comes with fires burning.
Morning comes with people singing.
Morning comes with alarm clocks ringing.
Morning comes with eggs cracking.
Morning comes with bacon sizzling.
Morning comes with letters dropping.
Morning comes with babies crying.

Gemma Nickel (9)
St Stephen's Primary School, Launceston

A WHOLE DAY

Daytime comes, with alarm dinging,
Daytime comes, with the shiny sun's gleam,
Daytime comes, with foodless bellies,
Daytime ends with a fabulous scorching sun.

Afternoon comes, with full up cramped bellies,
Afternoon comes, with a quick, quick play about,
Afternoon comes, with the clock moving extremely fast,
Afternoon ends, with a illuminous orange.

Night time comes, with lamp lights flickering,
Night time comes, with babies screaming wildly,
Night time comes, with dreams and nightmares put together,
Night time ends, with the beautiful, orange daytime.

Craig Charnock (9)
St Stephen's Primary School, Launceston

BEDTIME COMES

Bedtime comes with mum yelling
Bedtime comes with 'Just one more minute!'
Bedtime comes with scary nightmares
Bedtime comes with midnight horrors
Bedtime comes with Jamie snoring
Bedtime comes with beds creaking
Bedtime comes with people dreaming

Jamie Withers (10)
St Stephen's Primary School, Launceston

SAILING

On the boat we go whooshing, splashing
On the bow, up and down it goes
Big waves crashing in the side
Sail goes rumble!
Whistle, splash, whiz, whoosh, smash!
Stomach churning, ooohhh!
All calm now, mooring up now.
Clank! We're safe now on unrocky land.

Jake Doney (10)
St Stephen's Primary School, Launceston

PLAYING IN WATER!

Frogs croaking,
    Children swimming,
Fish darting,
    Legs itching,
Weeds tickling,
    Toddlers frowning,
Dads shouting,
    Bubble blowing,
Tadpoles stirring,
    Mums coughing,
Toads gargling,
    Dogs panting!

Leah Marie Ball (8)
St Stephen's Primary School, Launceston

COMING TO SCHOOL

Mothers running
Coats dragging
Babies screaming
Cars zooming
People rushing
Hearts racing
Dogs barking
Feet tamping
Children dawdling
Children racing

Briony Hemmings (9)
St Stephen's Primary School, Launceston

RAINY DAYS

Chocolate brown lipstick smudging on your wet lips,
on a rainy day.
Sludgy, mudgy water squelching in your big boots,
on a rainy day.
Blomp, domp, you're stamping in shiny glinting puddles,
on a rainy day.
Your soggy, damp hair is shaped into smooth spikes,
on a rainy day.
Grudgely, brudgely, you're feeling glum
(When will it be sunny again?)
on a rainy day.

Charlotte Cheeseman (10)
St Stephen's Primary School, Launceston

MUM'S BABY

Baby's crying
While mum's frying
Wants a bottle
Got the bottle
Down the milk goes
From its head to its toes
Now it's time for bed
Little sleepy head
The baby's snoring
How adoring
Then the baby bursts into tears
Mum comes then the crying clears
But now it's night
Don't let the bed bugs bite.

Genette Sproston (9)
St Stephen's Primary School, Launceston

A Canister Never Dies . . .

No one loves or cares for me -
There's no point telling lies,
But the truth is and the truth is this
That a canister never dies.

I floated unsteadily towards the horizon,
My body queasy and weak,
I wondered how the ocean got there,
Did some tap somewhere have a leak?

The icy, bitter wind whipped my cheeks cruelly,
The painful salt stung my eyes,
But as I said
A canister never ever *dies!*

After four years of gormless lone
I drifted on the golden sands of . . .
    Sennen!
My home.

Ruth Gallie (10)
Sennen Primary School

A Canister Never Dies

Once upon the sunlight clear,
A tiny canister full of fear,
In the sea by day by year,
When washed upon the beach right here.

There it laid hour by hour,
There it laid, it stayed and stayed,
Until one day it was picked up,
In a little drinking cup!

It was delivered to the school,
We took to it with a fall,
Inside it was a little passage,
It was a very interesting message.

Andrew Symons (11)
Sennen Primary School

GOD'S CREATION

God the king of all creation
Was the founder of our nation

From dirt and dust we were made
On the Earth we were laid

On the crest of the wave white horses stride
They gallop, manes furling full of pride

The fowl of air fly up to the stars
Then they return from travelling afar

The beast of the field stalk their prey
Then they retreat and feast away

Beautiful land so rich for the king
Not disturbed or awakened by any living thing

At last the time came
To bring sorrow and rain

But today thank your lucky star
To be where and who you are

When at last you pass on
You return to God fit and strong

Debbie Corlett (10)
Stratton Primary School

I WISH I WAS AN IGUANA

I   wish I was an iguana,
Sauntering slowly across the sand,

G   ently snoozing in the sun,
Laid on Earth by God's caring hand,

U   nder the canopy of leaves I lay safe,
Feasting heartily on swarms of bugs,

A   ble to change colour as quick as the wind,
Not scared of predators acting like thugs.

N   ever caught, never seen,
I have no friends, I live alone,

A   ble to cope with tough terrain,
My scales help me adapt to all weathers, so I don't need to moan!

Joely Ball (10)
Stratton Primary School

SQUIRRELS

Spying from my tree,
I watch the people passing by me,
Jumping from branch to branch,
Fingers pointing at me,
They stare at me,
With mouths wide open,
Performing on some rope, balance, climbing,
Audience sit amazed and astonished,
I found my hole and rest,
Until my next performance.

Samantha Webb (10)
Stratton Primary School

MY DREAM

Another history lesson
The teacher's voice floats away into the distance
As I rest my head my eyes feel droopy
I walk home through the sand
I can feel the dust through it
Instead of neat houses there's gigantic pyramids
The people are wearing white tunics
Camels are marching about, where's the cars?
All I can see is sand and men dragging big stones around
A boat is travelling down the river floating towards a pyramid

Suddenly I hear my teacher's voice
It was all just a dream.

Anna Cornish (11)
Stratton Primary School

HOSPITAL VISIT

Automatic doors opening to the corridor,
Past the worried visitors soothing their nerves,
Hearing them say, 'You look very well.'

A ward full of beds,
Like a line of gravestones,
Trapped in a bed like a box.

'You're looking better since I saw you last,'
Looking at the basket of fruit.

Colouring the ward with vases of flowers,
Pale faces as the nurses come to check their pulse,
Time to leave, waving goodbye.

Samantha Seymour-Smith (11)
Stratton Primary School

FOREST FIRE

Someone sets the paper alight
A person throws in logs and sticks
The campers get marshmallow
And roast them
Sticky marshmallow dripping into the fire.

It flickers in the darkness
Such a small fire leaves like petrol
Fuel for the fire
It catches a branch, then a tree
Then suddenly trees and trees are on fire
Now woods of trees
You can smell burning sap
And leaves all textures burnt
An inferno of trees all flames
No sound, no wildlife
Nothing.

Callum McEwan (10)
Stratton Primary School

JAGUARS

A sly character
Always darting from one place to another
Slipping into the undergrowth
Changing address from time to time
He stalks his prey carefully, getting ready to strike
Never having any friends, only the dealers fast and deadly
He catches his prey
Furtively exchanging boxes of drugs
He goes into the undergrowth again

Sam Granger (10)
Stratton Primary School

BONFIRE NIGHT

B onfire night is a perfect sight.
O ooo's and aaah's could be heard all around.
N ightly sky looking down on the flames.
F ire crackling gently.
I n and out the flames flicker.
R aging about then dying down quickly.
E xplosive decorations filling the pitch-black sky.

N othing compares with this wonderful sight.
I t seems like the colours are never going to fade.
G hostly noises all drowned out.
H appy faces all aglow.
T he shrieks of laughter echoing through the hills.

Maddie Chivers (10)
Stratton Primary School

SUMMERTIME

S un in your face giving you a tan
U nder your parasol keeping cool
M oulding the sand into your bucket
M aking sandcastles along the beach
E ating ice cream to keep cool
R unning in the wet sand into the sea.
T ime zooming past is if it was not there
I ce from the fridge melting so quickly
M any magnificent days of fun in the sea
E ach moment has now gone.

Alex Purcell (10)
Stratton Primary School

FUTURISTIC TALES

I wonder what it's gonna be like
In ten or twenty years?

Maybe there will be some Aliens
And acrobatic robots,

Also there could be steel dogs
With little aerials for tails,

All the transport would be air
In lots of big spaceships,

And you could go shopping
By just pressing a button,

In the parks there would be loads of . . .
Nothing, just a memory of a tree,

The animals would be gone
And pollution would take over,

All the world would be so shiny
With metal buildings gleaming,

And schools would not be
As education is not needed,

The only pet you could have is
The steel and lonely robot,

You would not have to do a thing
Because of computers' workings,

The air would be salty and sickly
From deadly black fumes,

But as we are not there yet,
You don't have to worry,

But still watch out
Because this is the way it'll turn out!

George Gifford (10)
Stratton Primary School

MIDNIGHT

M idnight is a magical thing,
I   ntriguing shadows creeping and crawling across the garden
D arkness has fallen, trees turn to monsters
N ight time stars flicker and twinkle in the moonlight
I   mages trick me as I doze
G leaming in the darkness I see a luminous moon
H owling winds seem like faraway cries
T   he midnight garden turns to morning.

Emma Henderson (11)
Stratton Primary School

TIGERS

Through day and night catching its prey.
It climbs over the broken branches.
Gathering speed it pounces from behind the tree.
Eating its prey head to toe it finally finishes its food.
Racing back up the tree it starts to rest and falls to sleep.
Sneaking, smelling and spying it starts a new morning.

Lynette Haydon (10)
Stratton Primary School

MY DAY

As I put on my new comfortable jumper
I think of people in India wearing old, filthy rags.
When I sit down to eat my tasty breakfast
I think of people in Africa very thin and starving.
As I play in the cold, sparkling sea
I think of people in cities who've never seen it before.
As I get out my homework to do for school
I think of children in the world who don't ever go to school.
I sit down to eat my tantalising tea
I think of a hand rummaging in dustbins searching for food.
As I get into my lovely, warm bed
I think of a man pulling a newspaper over his head.

Anya Perring (11)
Stratton Primary School

CONCENTRATION

'Take out your Geography book'
Oh dear! Here we go again,
'As the sea erodes one side . . .'
Meeting the Guides in my mind,
'And deposits sand . . .'
Vision of going to town with friends
'As the coast is torn away . . .'
I am aiming at the goal in Netball
'Pay attention'
Clicking her fingers at me
I shoot - a goal!

Leanne Stanbury (11)
Stratton Primary School

HOMELESS

I couldn't stand it at home anymore,
So I grabbed a few things and went out the door.
The park is where I would stay,
Every night and every day.
Everyone stares but just walks past,
They don't care if I'm down and outcast.
Out of fallen leaves I make a bed,
I'm dying of hunger, I need to be fed.
I look in the bins for something to eat,
A thrown-away sandwich and a sticky sweet.
When I'm bored I play on the swings,
And sometimes I wonder what the future will bring.
Some teenage boys walk up to me,
Their threatening stares make me want to flee.
I wish I hadn't run away,
Maybe next time at home I'll stay.

Kirsty Shadrick (10)
Stratton Primary School

DOLPHIN

She dives in every action she takes,
As the royal blue water smashes and breaks.
Never stops to think of danger,
In a rush taking no look to a stranger.

Dancing in the magnificent sunlight,
Making a turn away from a vicious fight.
Never really spiteful or unkind,
Always on the bright side of the ocean.

Katie Stanbury (11)
Stratton Primary School

BOY OF 10

Getting up slowly but still tired
Eating Frosties
Wondering what activities we'll do
Feeling bored while the teacher chatters
Trying to focus on what she's saying

Staring at the widescreen world
Cartoons are my favourite thing
Biking daily, loving every minute
Flying through the air free as a bird

Back to back fighting in the Judo Dojo
Disco dancing, hair spiked and gelled
Down to Earth, back to homework
Getting up slowly but still tired

Daniel Goodman (10)
Stratton Primary School

SNAKE

Undulating through the undergrowth,
He coils through the grass,
Then into a ball soaking in the sun.
His camouflage saves him from predators,
But how will his prey get away?
His fork-like tongue shaking,
He waits and waits.
He slithers towards his enemy.
He catches his prey.
It drops, its kill is successful.

Jonathan Down (10)
Stratton Primary School

I AM A VOLCANO

I am a huge volcano,
I sweep terror in the town,
Dispatching lava to boil the people,
And molten rock I send down.

I am a boiling volcano,
I put on a fireworks display,
Terrorising the inhabitants down below,
The show lasts all night and day.

I am a steaming volcano,
With a column of rising gas,
I rain pumice on my victims,
And pyroclastic flows filled with ash.

Tom Beswetherick (11)
Stratton Primary School

GOING THROUGH THE PAST

Terraced cottages all in a row
I walk along a cinder path
Moving for a horse and cart

Passing milk churns along the way
The muffin man greets me selling cakes
Eating them whilst they are warm
The corner shop full with sweets
With one penny I buy a cone for my luxury

Children playing buttons in the street
Open-topped cars passing by
Back to the time machine
Leaving the past behind

Bethany Miles (10)
Stratton Primary School

THE NOTE

It is invisible in its coat, as black as night,
Hovering like a humming bird when in flight,
Children following in delight,
Floating through the door and out of sight.

It brings joy to hearts everywhere,
Putting you in a mood for love and care,
Flowing smoothly out of its fairytale lair,
Gradually disappearing into thin air.

Tears come out and the future looks black,
Memories come flooding back,
But although I'm sad my brains I rack,
To find in what strength I lack.

It makes you realise we are all human beings,
Sad, happy, excited and mad,
The music note gives you a mixture of feelings.

Laura Gifford (11)
Stratton Primary School

HARRY POTTER

W hen I was a wizard
I   raced for the snitch in quiditch
Z   ap the world to stop, I want more presents for my birthday
A   n owl I got for my birthday when I zinged the world to start again
R   ecovered myself from the stone I tripped over
      and wrapped myself in my invisible cloak and flew off into the night
D   efending the sorcerer's stone in a life or death battle.

Tim Saxton (11)
Stratton Primary School

FRIENDS

Friends are always there for you,
They are precious as a gem but worth much more,
Making you happy when you're sad,
You turn to them when in need.

They are never cruel or mean to you,
The jokes they tell are comical,
We exchange smiles across the classroom,
You know what they're thinking without speaking.

We start with a giggle and end up screaming with laughter,
The teacher shouts, we sit stock still,
She looks away, we wink to each other.

Laura Chidley (10)
Stratton Primary School

CRAB

Feet crashing into the water beside me
Scuttling away, snapping at toes
Finding my cave in the swell

I am hungry so I look for food
Look there, a tiny shoal of fish
With my razor-sharp claws I grab one

I rip my prey with conviction
My jaws work busily to strip the flesh
Satisfied I donate the carcass to the sea

Jim Scown (11)
Stratton Primary School

I WISH I WAS A HORSE

Helping the farmers plough their fields,
Putting seeds in for harvest.

Pulling carriages, exercising horses,
Carrying milk for the people.

Chasing the hunt,
Setting the dogs on the run.

Riding fast giving lots of pleasure,
Making little children laugh.

Jockeys fighting to win the race,
Finding Red Shadow's come first place.

Ellen Sanders (11)
Stratton Primary School

A LAVA LAMP

A   lava lamp relaxed the mind

L   eaving all your troubles behind
A   mazing thoughts plunder in your head
V   anishing into cosmic forms
A   stonishing shapes around in the glass

L   ava melting into smouldering liquid
A   pertures forming and being filled in
M   agma mixtures add to the molten rock
P   eace should soon set in again

Bethany Foot (11)
Stratton Primary School

FOOTPRINTS

I know you get discouraged
Because I am so small
And always leave my footprints
On the kitchen floor

But every day I am growing
I'll be all grown up some day
And all the prints that I did
Will definitely fade away

So here's another load
Just so you can recall
Exactly how my feet looked
When I was so very small

PS: If they don't fade I don't care

Elliot Thomas Berry (10)
The Bishop's CE Primary School

THE WITCH

There in the middle of the deep, dark, scary woods
Stood a witch.
Her eyes red as red could be.
Her hair crawling with spiders.
Her nose as sharp as a sword.
Her mouth was blood red.
Her hat so pointed that the top sparkled in the moonlight.
Her cloak black as the night.
Her hands thin and bony.
Her shoes were needle-sharp.
She is the sort of person who will give you nightmares forever.
She will send shivers down your back.

Romey Vassell (9)
The Bishop's CE Primary School

I'M SORRY

I'm sorry I had muddy feet
And walked them on the floor
When I came through I made you scream
And run straight out the door.

I'm sorry I had to break something
And that something was your mop
I'm very, very sorry
I'll get a new one at the shop.

I'm sorry I painted your shirt
I'm sorry I scared your cat
I'm sorry I broke your sharpener
I'm sorry I ripped your mat
I'm sorry for all this trouble.

Bang! Oops, sorry!

Amelia Best (9)
The Bishop's CE Primary School

WITCH

My witch is called Sabrina,
She lives in a normal house with purple curtains.
My witch has long blonde hair and shiny blue eyes,
She has dark red lips.
My witch wears a strap top and a purple mini leather skirt.
She has big high heels and she has her ears pierced nine times,
My witch casts spells on other children like Libby.
She has four animals, a fish, a horse, a cat and a dog,
My witch is kind, clever, beautiful and smart.
She has long red fingernails.
My witch is so nice that I would make friends with her straight away.

Philippa Higman (9)
The Bishop's CE Primary School

EARLY IN THE MORNING

Early in the morning as the sun rises up,
People sip their tea from their early morning cup.

Early in the morning people wake up from their sleep,
People's alarm clocks go *beep, beep, beep.*

Early in the morning as the birds begin to stir,
Everyone's cats are beginning to *purr.*

Early in the morning as the rooster starts to call,
I get out of my bed and try not to fall.

Early in the morning when I'm ready for school,
My mum says I'm pretty and really, really cool.

I'm at school now, I say bye to my mum,
I have to start my work, a new day has begun.

Cara Searle (8)
Threemilestone Primary School

A SPACE VOYAGE

5, 4, 3, 2, 1,
Ignition!
Starting off slowly
Getting faster, faster, faster
And faster
Until it's a microscopic speck in the distance.
Booster rockets burning millions of gallons of fuel,
Searching through the universe for distant planets.

Ben Chandler (10)
Trevisker Primary School

A STAR

A bright star -
   Lighting up the dark,
A dull star -
   A puny little mark.

A big star -
   Which looks so great to me,
A small star -
   But bright enough to see.

A burning star -
   About to disappear,
A dead star -
   Which will never reappear.

Tom Rogers (10)
Trevisker Primary School

A SPACE VOYAGE

Five, four, three, two, one,
Blast-off!
Pushing slowly upwards,
Faster and faster,
Until it's a tiny speck in the sky.
Guzzling fuel,
Searching through the solar system,
Searching for another kind of life.

Alfie Chapman (9)
Trevisker Primary School

Our Mission

The Earth's atmosphere has cracked up,
Its countries are starting to burn,
We have to find a new home,
To escape from this furious heat.

We are setting off to another galaxy,
Our mission to save human life,
Our rocket is called 'Star Ship',
In a rocket there's room for so few.

Blasting through space
To a place no one has seen before,
Our hopes for a future
Where everyone will be safe.

Natalie Taylor (9)
Trevisker Primary School

A Space Voyage

Five, four, three, two, one,
Blast-off!
Starting off sluggish,
getting quicker and quicker
and quicker.
Until it's a little speck in the sky.
Blasting rockets,
gulping fuel,
looking for somewhere
no man has ever been before.

Tom Wood (10)
Trevisker Primary School

JOURNEY THROUGH SPACE

Out in the dark
I saw a bright spark,
It puzzled me
What could it be?

Where was it from?
Where was it going?
I don't know,
Or what even to think.

Then it came to me,
It was a star
That just burst
Come from afar!

Jocelyn Stevenson (10)
Trevisker Primary School

MY JOURNEY TO PLUTO

As I travel far and wide,
I pass by planets as I ride,
When I soar through the distant skies,
See many stars about to die,
Jupiter and Saturn,
Giant planets, moons and rings,
Is there life? Are there patterns?
I'm amazed by all these things!

Patrick Intorre (10)
Trevisker Primary School

MY JOURNEY TO OTHER GALAXIES

As I travel far and wide,
I pass by planets in the sky.
The spacecraft gives a bumpy ride,
As I run away from a star about to die.

This spacecraft is the best,
Looking back at the tiny sun,
For now I have to rest,
Looking forward, I see galaxies.

Will this mission never end?
I travel past galaxies but no life.
Soon I will have nowhere to go,
For I have no return to Earth.

Cara Elizabeth Vickers (10)
Trevisker Primary School